KIKKOMAN

Oriental
Cooking

KIKKOMAN BRINGS THE ORIENT HOME

Oriental cuisine may be many centuries old, but its distinctive flavors and cooking methods are timeless and well suited for those who have less time to spend in the kitchen. Whether you're an experienced cook or just starting out, you'll enjoy sampling the culinary heritage featured here. This book is filled with delicious, easy-to-prepare recipes—appetizers, main dishes, salads and side dishes—that are perfect for everyday meals and entertaining.

For over 350 years, Asian cooks have relied on the superior quality of naturally brewed Kikkoman Soy Sauce to artfully season their favorite dishes. Kikkoman's six-month brewing process, using only natural ingredients, creates a unique flavor, aroma and color that can't be duplicated.

If you're concerned about the level of sodium in your diet, you'll appreciate Kikkoman Lite Soy Sauce. It has 40 percent less salt, yet retains all the tastiness and aroma of naturally brewed soy sauce because the salt is extracted *after* brewing.

Kikkoman Soy Sauce is the prime ingredient in all of the convenient and tasty sauces featured in thes full-flavored recipes. The distinctiv flavor of teriyaki is easy to achiev with Kikkoman Teriyaki Sauce. It's delicious shortcut to many othe Oriental specialties, too. You'll als find Kikkoman Teriyaki Baste Glaze produces a rich, lush flavor i virtually no time, whether you broi grill, bake or roast.

Easy-to-use Kikkoman Stir-Fr Sauce, with its authentic flavo eliminates the fuss of making a sti fry sauce from scratch. Kikkoma Sweet & Sour Sauce adds just th right amount of traditional Chines flavor, whether it's used as an ingre dient or as a tasty dipping sauce.

Although a variety of familiar cook ing techniques are used in preparin Oriental dishes, stir-frying, the mos popular technique, is feature throughout this book. Before you begin, take a few minutes to read th following information. Stir-frying i easily mastered, and these helpfu guidelines will enhance your enjoy ment of these wonderful dishes.

Stir-frying involves the rapid cook ing of ingredients in a small amoun of oil over high heat for a few min utes. In addition to saving time, th

uick cooking preserves the nutri-
nts, flavors, textures and colors of
od. Stir-frying can be divided into
vo separate steps: the preparing of
gredients and the actual cooking.

is essential to have all the ingredi-
nts prepared in advance. This
eans all cleaning, cutting, measur-
g, combining, etc. Stir-frying pro-
eeds so quickly that there is no
me to do anything else once cook-
g begins. When cutting meats and
egetables, make the pieces a uni-
rm shape and size to ensure even
oking. Otherwise, one ingredient
ay overcook while others remain
ndercooked. To help seal in the
atural juices and increase flavor,
e meat should be lightly coated
ith a sauce before cooking.

Vhen you're ready to begin, place a
ok or large skillet over high heat.
reheating the pan prevents the
od from sticking.) When a drop of
ater added to the pan sizzles, the
an is sufficiently hot. Next add the
il, swirling to coat the inside of the
an; heat until the oil is hot, about
0 seconds. Now the ingredients
an be added.

Stir-fry the meat first and remove.
Then add the vegetables, beginning
with those that take the longest to
cook. Briskly toss and stir with a flat
metal or wooden spatula. Be sure to
keep the food in constant motion.
This ensures that all surfaces are
quickly coated with hot oil to seal in
the flavorings, and also to prevent
overcooking or burning. To main-
tain the characteristic Chinese
tender-crisp quality, serve stir-fried
dishes immediately.

The best oils to use for stir-frying
are vegetable oils that can withstand
intense heat without smoking. Peanut oil, corn oil and soybean oil are
excellent choices.

We hope you enjoy all of the Oriental specialties in this book. Simply
follow the recipes closely and you'll
be an Oriental chef in virtually no
time at all. And once you've mastered the basics of Oriental cooking,
creating your own classics is easy.
All you need are quality ingredients,
complementary flavors and timely
preparation. Don't be afraid to try
your own ideas—that's how great
chefs are born!

APPETIZERS

MEAT-FILLED ORIENTAL PANCAKES

Makes 2 dozen appetizers

    6 Oriental Pancakes (recipe follows)
    1 tablespoon cornstarch
    3 tablespoons Kikkoman Soy Sauce
    1 tablespoon dry sherry
  3/4 pound ground beef
  1/2 pound ground pork
  2/3 cup chopped green onions and tops
    1 teaspoon minced fresh ginger root
    1 clove garlic, pressed

Prepare Oriental Pancakes on page 6. Combine
cornstarch, soy sauce and sherry in large bowl. Add
beef, pork, green onions, ginger and garlic; mix until
thoroughly combined. Spread 1/2 cup meat mixture
evenly over each pancake, leaving about a 1/2-inch
border on 1 side. Starting with opposite side, roll up
pancake jelly-roll fashion. Place rolls, seam side down,
in single layer, on heatproof plate; place plate on
steamer rack. Set rack in large pot or wok of boiling
water. Cover and steam 15 minutes. (For best results,
steam all rolls at the same time.) Just before serving,
cut rolls diagonally into quarters. Arrange on serving
platter and serve hot.

頭枱食譜

CRISPY WONTONS

Makes 10 appetizer servings

3/4 **pound ground pork**
  8 **water chestnuts, finely
     chopped**
1/4 **cup finely chopped green
     onions and tops**
  1 **tablespoon Kikkoman Soy
     Sauce**
1/2 **teaspoon salt**
  1 **teaspoon cornstarch**
1/2 **teaspoon grated fresh ginger
     root**
  1 **package (1 lb.) wonton skins
     Vegetable oil for frying
     Tomato catsup and hot
        mustard *or* Kikkoman Sweet
        & Sour Sauce**

Combine pork, water chestnuts, green
onions, soy sauce, salt, cornstarch
and ginger in medium bowl; mix well.
Place 1/2 teaspoonful pork mixture in
center of each wonton skin. Fold wonton skin over filling to form a triangle.
Turn top of triangle down to meet
fold. Turn over; moisten 1 corner with
water. Overlap opposite corner over
moistened corner; press firmly. Heat
oil in wok or large saucepan over
medium-high heat to 375°F. Deep fry
wontons, a few at a time, 2 to 3 minutes, or until brown and crispy. Drain
on paper towels. Serve warm with catsup and mustard or sweet & sour
sauce, as desired.

ORIENTAL PANCAKES:

Beat *4 eggs* in large bowl with wire
whisk. Combine *1/2 cup water, 3 tablespoons cornstarch, 2 teaspoons Kikkoman Soy Sauce* and *1/2 teaspoon
sugar;* pour into eggs and beat well.
Heat an 8-inch omelet or crepe pan
over medium heat. Brush bottom of
pan with *1/2 teaspoon vegetable oil;* reduce heat to low. Beat egg mixture;
pour *1/4 cupful* into skillet, lifting and
tipping pan from side to side to form a
thin round pancake. Cook about 1 to
1 1/2 minutes, or until firm. Carefully
lift with spatula and transfer to a sheet
of waxed paper. Continue procedure,
adding *1/2 teaspoon oil* to pan for each
pancake. Makes 6 pancakes.

EGG DROP SOUP

Makes about 12 cups

  3 **quarts water**
  9 **chicken bouillon cubes**
1/3 **cup Kikkoman Soy Sauce**
  6 **eggs, well beaten**
1 1/2 **cups finely chopped green
     onions and tops**

Bring water to boil in large saucepan;
add bouillon cubes and stir until dis-
solved. Stir in soy sauce; return to
boil. Remove from heat; add eggs all
at once, stirring rapidly in 1 direction
with spoon. (Eggs will separate to
form fine threads.) Stir in green onions. Serve immediately.

Crispy Wontons

EMPRESS CHICKEN WINGS

Makes 4 to 6 appetizer servings

1½ pounds chicken wings (about 8 wings)
3 tablespoons Kikkoman Soy Sauce
1 tablespoon dry sherry
1 tablespoon minced fresh ginger root
1 clove garlic, minced
2 tablespoons vegetable oil
¼ to ⅓ cup cornstarch
⅔ cup water
2 green onions and tops, cut diagonally into thin slices
1 teaspoon slivered fresh ginger root

Disjoint chicken wings; discard tips (or save for stock). Combine soy sauce, sherry, minced ginger and garlic in large bowl; stir in chicken. Cover and refrigerate 1 hour, stirring occasionally. Remove chicken; reserve marinade. Heat oil in large skillet over medium heat. Lightly coat chicken pieces with cornstarch; add to skillet and brown slowly on all sides. Remove chicken; drain off fat. Stir water and reserved marinade into same skillet. Add chicken; sprinkle green onions and slivered ginger evenly over chicken. Cover and simmer 5 minutes, or until chicken is tender.

Empress Chicken Wings

SPRING ROLLS

Makes 8 appetizer servings

- 1/2 pound ground pork
- 1 teaspoon Kikkoman Soy Sauce
- 1 teaspoon dry sherry
- 1/2 teaspoon garlic salt
- 2 tablespoons vegetable oil
- 3 cups fresh bean sprouts
- 1/2 cup sliced onion
- 1 tablespoon Kikkoman Soy Sauce
- 1 tablespoon cornstarch
- 3/4 cup water, divided
- 8 sheets egg roll skins
- 1/2 cup prepared biscuit mix
- 1 egg, beaten
  Vegetable oil for frying
  Hot mustard, tomato catsup and Kikkoman Soy Sauce

Combine pork, 1 teaspoon soy sauce, sherry and garlic salt; mix well. Let stand 15 minutes. Heat 2 tablespoons oil in hot wok or large skillet over medium-high heat; brown pork mixture in hot oil. Add bean sprouts, onion and 1 tablespoon soy sauce. Stir-fry until vegetables are tender-crisp; drain and cool. Dissolve cornstarch in 1/4 cup water. Place about 1/3 cupful pork mixture on lower half of egg roll skin. Moisten left and right edges with cornstarch mixture. Fold bottom edge up to just cover filling. Fold left and right edges 1/2 inch over; roll up jelly-roll fashion. Moisten top edge with cornstarch mixture and seal. Complete all rolls. Combine biscuit mix, egg and remaining 1/2 cup water in small bowl; dip each roll in batter. Heat oil for frying in wok or large saucepan over medium-high heat to 370°F. Deep fry rolls, a few at a time, in hot oil 5 to 7 minutes, or until golden brown, turning often. Drain on paper towels. Slice each roll into 4 pieces. Serve with mustard, catsup and soy sauce as desired.

SHRIMP TERIYAKI

Makes 10 appetizer servings

- 1/2 cup Kikkoman Soy Sauce
- 2 tablespoons sugar
- 1 tablespoon vegetable oil
- 1 1/2 teaspoons cornstarch
- 1 clove garlic, crushed
- 1 teaspoon minced fresh ginger root
- 2 tablespoons water
- 2 pounds medium-size raw shrimp, peeled and deveined

Blend soy sauce, sugar, oil, cornstarch, garlic, ginger and water in small saucepan. Simmer, stirring constantly, until thickened, about 1 minute; cool. Coat shrimp with sauce; drain off excess. Place on rack of broiler pan. Broil 5 inches from heat source 3 to 4 minutes on each side, or until shrimp are opaque and cooked. Serve immediately with wooden picks.

SESAME CHEESE CRACKERS

Makes 8 appetizer servings

- 1 cup all-purpose flour
- 1/2 teaspoon salt
- 1/8 teaspoon ground red pepper (cayenne)
- 6 tablespoons cold butter or margarine
- 1 cup (4 oz.) finely grated Cheddar cheese
- 1/4 cup sesame seed, toasted
- 1/2 teaspoon Kikkoman Soy Sauce
- 4 1/2 to 7 1/2 teaspoons ice-cold water

Combine flour, salt and pepper in medium bowl; cut in butter until mixture resembles coarse crumbs. Stir in cheese and sesame seed. Combine soy sauce and 3 teaspoons water; stir into dry ingredients. Add more water, a little at a time, mixing lightly until dough begins to stick together. Turn out dough and press together on lightly floured board or pastry cloth; roll out to 1/8-inch thickness. Cut dough into 2 × 1-inch rectangles with pastry wheel or knife. Place on lightly greased baking sheets and bake at 400°F. 8 to 10 minutes, or until lightly browned. Remove crackers to rack to cool.

CANTONESE MEATBALLS

Makes 6 to 8 appetizer servings

- 1 can (20 oz.) pineapple chunks in syrup
- 3 tablespoons brown sugar, packed
- 5 tablespoons Kikkoman Teriyaki Sauce, divided
- 1 tablespoon vinegar
- 1 tablespoon tomato catsup
- 1 pound lean ground beef
- 2 tablespoons instant minced onion
- 2 tablespoons cornstarch
- 1/4 cup water

Drain pineapple; reserve syrup. Combine syrup, brown sugar, 3 tablespoons teriyaki sauce, vinegar and catsup; set aside. Mix beef with remaining 2 tablespoons teriyaki sauce and onion; shape into 20 meatballs. Brown meatballs in large skillet; drain off excess fat. Pour syrup mixture over meatballs; simmer 10 minutes, stirring occasionally. Dissolve cornstarch in water; stir into skillet with pineapple. Cook and stir until sauce thickens and pineapple is heated through.

Clear Japanese Soup with Sesame Cheese Crackers

CLEAR JAPANESE SOUP

Makes about 6 cups

1 1/2 quarts chicken broth
1/3 cup dry sherry
1 1/2 teaspoons Kikkoman Soy
   Sauce
1 lemon, thinly sliced

Garnishes:
5 to 6 fresh mushrooms, sliced
2 green onions and tops, sliced
   diagonally
1 carrot, very thinly sliced

Bring broth to simmer in large sauce-pan. Add sherry and soy sauce; simmer 2 to 3 minutes. Ladle soup into small bowls; float a lemon slice in each bowl. Arrange garnishes on tray and add to soup as desired.

PRAWNS-IN-SHELL

Makes 8 appetizer servings

1 pound large raw prawns
2 tablespoons dry white wine,
   divided
1/2 teaspoon grated fresh ginger
   root
1/4 cup vegetable oil
2 tablespoons coarsely chopped
   green onions and tops
1 teaspoon coarsely chopped
   fresh ginger root
1 clove garlic, chopped
2 small red chili peppers,*
   coarsely chopped
1 tablespoon sugar
3 tablespoons tomato catsup
2 tablespoons Kikkoman Soy
   Sauce
1/2 teaspoon cornstarch

Wash and devein prawns; do not peel. Cut prawns diagonally into halves; place in medium bowl. Sprinkle 1 tablespoon wine and grated ginger over prawns. Heat oil in hot wok or large skillet over high heat. Add prawns; stir-fry until completely pink or red. Add green onions, chopped ginger, garlic and chili peppers; stir-fry only until onions are tender. Combine sugar, catsup, soy sauce, remaining 1 tablespoon wine and cornstarch; pour into pan. Cook and stir until sauce boils and thickens. Serve immediately. Garnish as desired.

*Wear rubber gloves when working with chilis and wash hands in warm soapy water. Avoid touching face or eyes.

SESAME PORK TIDBITS WITH SWEET & SOUR SAUCE

Makes about 3 dozen appetizers

1 1/2 pounds boneless pork loin
1/2 cup cornstarch
1/4 cup Kikkoman Teriyaki Sauce
3 tablespoons sesame seed,
   lightly toasted
   Sweet & Sour Sauce (recipe
   follows)
3 cups vegetable oil

Trim excess fat from pork; cut into 1-inch cubes and set aside. Thoroughly combine cornstarch, teriyaki sauce and sesame seed in medium bowl (mixture will be very stiff). Stir in pork cubes; let stand 30 minutes. Meanwhile, prepare Sweet & Sour Sauce; keep warm. Heat oil in medium saucepan over medium-high heat to 300°F. Add 1/3 of the pork cubes and cook, stirring constantly, until golden brown, about 2 minutes. Remove and drain thoroughly on paper towels. Repeat with remaining pork. Serve immediately with warm Sweet & Sour Sauce.

SWEET & SOUR SAUCE:
Combine *1/4 cup sugar, 1/4 cup vinegar, 1/4 cup catsup, 1/4 cup water, 1 tablespoon Kikkoman Teriyaki Sauce and 1 1/2 teaspoons cornstarch* in small saucepan. Cook over high heat, stirring constantly, until thickened.

Prawns-in-Shell

STEAMED STUFFED ZUCCHINI ROUNDS

Makes 6 to 8 appetizer servings

4 zucchini, 6 to 7 inches long,
 about 1 1/2 inches in
 diameter
1/2 cup Kikkoman Teriyaki Sauce
1/2 pound ground beef
1/2 cup dry bread crumbs
1/4 cup minced green onions and
 tops

Trim off and discard ends of zucchin
cut crosswise into 3/4-inch length:
Scoop out flesh, leaving about 1/8
inch shell on sides and bottoms; re
serve flesh. Place zucchini rounds i
large plastic bag; pour in teriyak
sauce. Press air out of bag; tie top se
curely. Marinate 30 minutes, turnin
bag over occasionally. Meanwhile
coarsely chop zucchini flesh; reserv
1/2 cup. Remove zucchini rounds fron
marinade; reserve 1/4 cup marinade
Combine reserved marinade wit
beef, bread crumbs, green onions an
1/2 cup reserved zucchini flesh. Fil
each round with about 2 teaspoonfu
beef mixture. Place rounds, filled sid
up, on steamer rack. Set rack in larg
pot or wok of boiling water. (Do not a
low water level to reach zucchini
Cover and steam 6 minutes, or unt
zucchini rounds are tender-crisp whe
pierced with fork. Serve immediatel

WAIKIKI APPETIZERS

Makes 6 to 8 appetizer servings

1 1/2 pounds bulk pork sausage
1 can (20 oz.) pineapple chunks
 in syrup
1/2 cup brown sugar, packed
1/4 cup lemon juice
2 tablespoons cornstarch
2 tablespoons Kikkoman Soy
 Sauce
1/2 cup chopped green pepper
1/2 cup drained maraschino
 cherries

Shape sausage into 1/2- to 3/4-inch
balls. Place in single layer in baking
pan. Bake in 400°F. oven 25 minutes,
or until cooked; drain on paper towels. Meanwhile, drain pineapple; reserve syrup. Add enough water to
syrup to measure 1 cup; combine
with brown sugar, lemon juice, cornstarch and soy sauce in large saucepan. Cook and stir until sauce boils
and thickens. Fold in green pepper,
cherries, pineapple chunks and
drained cooked sausage. To serve,
turn into chafing dish.

Top: Steamed Stuffed Zucchini Round
Bottom: Waikiki Appetizer

HOT & SOUR SOUP

Makes about 5 cups

1 can (10½ oz.) condensed
  chicken broth
2 soup cans water
1 can (4 oz.) sliced mushrooms
2 tablespoons cornstarch
2 tablespoons Kikkoman Soy
  Sauce
2 tablespoons distilled white
  vinegar
½ teaspoon Tabasco pepper
  sauce
1 egg, beaten
2 green onions and tops,
  chopped

Combine chicken broth, water, mushrooms, cornstarch, soy sauce, vinegar and pepper sauce in medium saucepan. Bring to boil over high heat, stirring constantly, until slightly thickened. Gradually pour egg into boiling soup, stirring constantly in 1 direction. Remove from heat; stir in green onions. Garnish with additional chopped green onions or cilantro, as desired. Serve immediately.

Hot & Sour Soup

SAUCY SHRIMP

Makes 6 appetizer servings

1/2 pound medium-size raw shrimp
1/4 cup Kikkoman Teriyaki Baste
& Glaze
2 tablespoons dry sherry
1 tablespoon lime juice
1 tablespoon sliced green onions
and tops
3 to 4 drops Tabasco pepper
sauce

Peel, devein and butterfly shrimp. Combine teriyaki baste & glaze, sherry, lime juice, green onions and pepper sauce in medium bowl; stir in shrimp. Cover; refrigerate at least 1 hour, stirring occasionally. Remove shrimp and place on rack of broiler pan. Broil 2 to 3 minutes on each side, or until shrimp are opaque and cooked. Serve immediately with wooden picks.

POLYNESIAN KABOBS

Makes 25 appetizers

1 can (20 oz.) pineapple chunks
in syrup
6 tablespoons Kikkoman Soy
Sauce
3 tablespoons honey
1 tablespoon dry sherry
1 teaspoon grated orange peel
1/8 teaspoon garlic powder
2 pounds cooked ham, cut into
25 cubes (1 inch)
1 pound thickly sliced bacon
25 large stuffed olives
25 cherry tomatoes

Drain pineapple; reserve syrup. Blend syrup, soy sauce, honey, sherry, orange peel and garlic powder in large bowl; stir in ham cubes. Cover; refrigerate 1 hour, stirring occasionally. Cut each bacon slice crosswise in half; wrap pineapple chunks with halved bacon slices. Thread bamboo or metal skewers with a wrapped pineapple chunk, an olive, another wrapped pineapple, a marinated ham cube and a cherry tomato. Place skewers on rack of broiler pan; brush with marinade. Broil 3 to 4 inches from heat source 2 to 3 minutes on each side, or until bacon is crisp.

SHRIMP WITH SWEET & SOUR SAUCE

Makes 10 appetizer servings

- 2 pounds medium-size raw shrimp
- 2/3 cup vinegar
- 2/3 cup brown sugar, packed
- 2 teaspoons cornstarch
- 2 tablespoons Kikkoman Soy Sauce
- 1 cup water
- 1/2 teaspoon Tabasco pepper sauce

Peel shrimp, leaving tails on; devein Simmer in large pot of boiling salted water 5 minutes; drain and cool. Wrap and refrigerate. Combine vinegar brown sugar, cornstarch, soy sauce and water in small saucepan. Simmer stirring constantly, until thickened about 1 minute; stir in pepper sauce Pour into chafing dish; serve with cold shrimp.

BITS O' TERIYAKI CHICKEN

Makes 6 appetizer servings

- 1/2 cup Kikkoman Teriyaki Sauce
- 1 teaspoon sugar
- 2 whole chicken breasts, skinned and boned
- 1 teaspoon cornstarch
- 1 tablespoon water
- 1 tablespoon vegetable oil
- 2 tablespoons sesame seed, toasted

Combine teriyaki sauce and sugar in small bowl. Cut chicken into 1-inch pieces; stir into teriyaki sauce mixture. Marinate 30 minutes, stirring occasionally. Remove chicken; reserve 2 tablespoons marinade. Combine reserved marinade, cornstarch and water in small bowl; set aside. Heat oil in hot wok or large skillet over medium-high heat. Add chicken and sesame seed; stir-fry 2 minutes. Stir in cornstarch mixture. Cook and stir until mixture boils and thickens and chicken is tender, about 1 minute. Turn into chafing dish or onto serving platter. Serve warm with wooden picks.

TOASTED SESAME CHEESE SPREAD

Makes 4 to 6 appetizer servings

- 2 tablespoons Kikkoman Soy Sauce
- 1 package (3 oz.) cream cheese
- 4 teaspoons sesame seed, toasted
- Assorted crackers

Pour soy sauce over cream cheese block in small dish, turning over several times to coat all sides. Cover; refrigerate 2 hours, turning cheese block over often. Remove cheese block from soy sauce and roll in sesame seed. Refrigerate until ready to serve with crackers.

Glazed Ginger Chicken

GLAZED GINGER CHICKEN

Makes 8 appetizer servings

1 tablespoon sesame seed, toasted
1 tablespoon cornstarch
5 tablespoons Kikkoman Soy Sauce
3 tablespoons plum jam
1 tablespoon minced fresh ginger root
1 clove garlic, pressed
8 small chicken thighs (about 2 pounds)

Cut eight 8-inch squares of aluminum foil; set aside. Combine sesame seed, cornstarch, soy sauce, plum jam, ginger and garlic in small saucepan. Bring to boil over medium heat, stirring constantly. Remove from heat and cool slightly. Stir in thighs, a few at a time, to coat each piece well. Place 1 thigh, skin side up, on each foil square. Divide and spoon remaining sauce evenly over thighs. Fold ends of foil to form a package; crease and fold down to secure well. Place foil bundles, seam side up, in single layer, on steamer rack. Set rack in large pot or wok of boiling water. (Do not allow water level to reach bundles.) Cover and steam 30 minutes, or until chicken is tender. Garnish as desired. Serve immediately.

SPICY PORK STRIPS

Makes 6 to 8 appetizer servings

1 pound boneless pork chops,
   1/2 inch thick
1/3 cup Kikkoman Soy Sauce
1/4 cup minced green onions and
   tops
1 tablespoon sugar
1 tablespoon sesame seed,
   toasted
3 tablespoons water
1 1/2 teaspoons minced fresh ginger
   root
1 teaspoon Tabasco pepper
   sauce
1 clove garlic, minced

Slice pork into 1/4-inch-thick strips, about 4 inches long. Thread onto metal or bamboo skewers, keeping meat as flat as possible. Arrange skewers in large shallow pan. Blend soy sauce, green onions, sugar, sesame seed, water, ginger, pepper sauce and garlic, stirring until sugar dissolves. Pour mixture evenly over skewers; turn over to coat all sides. Let stand 30 minutes, turning skewers over occasionally. Reserving marinade, remove skewers and place on rack of broiler pan; brush with reserved marinade. Broil 3 minutes, or until pork is tender, turning once and basting with additional marinade.

BEEF KUSHISASHI

Makes 10 to 12 appetizer servings

1/2 cup Kikkoman Soy Sauce
1/4 cup chopped green onions and
   tops
2 tablespoons sugar
1 tablespoon vegetable oil
1 1/2 teaspoons cornstarch
1 clove garlic, pressed
1 teaspoon grated fresh ginger
   root
2 1/2 pounds boneless beef sirloin
   steak

Blend soy sauce, green onions, sugar, oil, cornstarch, garlic and ginger in small saucepan. Simmer, stirring constantly, until thickened, about 1 minute; cool. Cover and set aside. Slice beef into 1/8-inch-thick strips about 4 inches long and 1 inch wide. Thread onto bamboo or metal skewers keeping meat as flat as possible; brush both sides of beef with sauce. Place skewers on rack of broiler pan; broil to desired degree of doneness.

Top: Spicy Pork Strips
Bottom: Beef Kushisashi

KOREAN BEEF STICKS

Makes 6 to 8 appetizer servings

1 pound boneless beef sirloin
   steak, about 1/2 inch thick
1/4 cup Kikkoman Soy Sauce
1 tablespoon sesame seed,
   toasted
1 tablespoon water
2 teaspoons sugar
1/2 teaspoon Tabasco pepper
   sauce
1 clove garlic, pressed

MICROWAVE DIRECTIONS:
Slice beef into 1/4-inch-thick strips,
each about 4 to 5 inches long. Thread
onto bamboo skewers, keeping meat
as flat as possible. Arrange skewers in
large shallow pan. Blend soy sauce,
sesame seed, water, sugar, pepper
sauce and garlic, stirring until sugar
dissolves. Pour mixture evenly over
skewers; turn over to coat all sides. Let
stand 30 minutes, turning skewers
over occasionally. Remove skewers
from marinade; place half on flat,
microwave-safe plate. Microwave on
High 30 seconds. Turn skewers over
and bring skewers from outside of
plate to center. Microwave on High 30
seconds (for rare), or to desired degree of doneness. Repeat procedure
with remaining skewers.

PARCHMENT-WRAPPED CHICKEN

Makes 8 appetizer servings

2 whole chicken breasts, skinned
   and boned
3 tablespoons Kikkoman Soy
   Sauce
1 teaspoon ginger juice*
1/4 teaspoon sugar
   Boiling water
1/2 pound fresh bean sprouts
6 green onions and tops, cut into
   2-inch lengths and slivered
1/3 cup chopped toasted walnuts

Cut eight 8-inch squares of parchment paper; set aside. Cut chicken
into thin, narrow strips, about 3
inches long. Combine soy sauce, ginger juice and sugar in large bowl; stir
in chicken. Let stand 30 minutes.
Meanwhile, pour boiling water over
bean sprouts; let stand 1 minute.
Drain; cool under cold water and
drain well. Thoroughly toss chicken
mixture with bean sprouts, green onions and walnuts. Place about 1/2 cupful chicken mixture in center of each
parchment square. Fold bottom point
of parchment over filling; crease just
below filling and fold point over and
under filling. Fold side points over filling, overlapping slightly. Crease paper to hold folds. Fold remaining
corner down so point extends below
bottom of bundle; tuck this point be-
tween folded sides. Crease paper to
hold folds. Repeat with remaining
parchment squares. Place bundles,
seam side down, in single layer, on
steamer rack. Set rack in large pot or
wok of boiling water. (Do not allow water level to reach bundles.) Cover and
steam about 7 minutes, or until
chicken is tender. Serve immediately.

*Peel fresh ginger root, then squeeze
through garlic press.

YAKITORI

Makes 4 dozen appetizers

3 pounds chicken breasts
1 bunch green onions, cut into
    1-inch lengths
1 pound chicken livers, trimmed,
    rinsed and drained
1 cup Kikkoman Soy Sauce
1/4 cup sugar
1 tablespoon vegetable oil
2 cloves garlic, pressed
3/4 teaspoon ground ginger

Remove skin and bones from chicken, keeping meat in 1 piece; cut into 1-inch lengths. Thread chicken pieces onto metal or bamboo skewers with green onions (spear through side) and chicken livers. Arrange skewers in large shallow pan. Blend soy sauce, sugar, oil, garlic and ginger; pour mixture over skewers. Brush each skewer thoroughly with sauce. Cover and refrigerate about 1 hour, turning skewers over occasionally. Reserving marinade, remove skewers and place on rack of broiler pan. Broil 5 inches from heat source 3 minutes on each side, or until chicken is tender; brush with reserved marinade after turning.

MONGOLIAN ALMONDS

Makes 1 cup

1 cup whole natural almonds
2 tablespoons Kikkoman Teriyaki
    Sauce
1 teaspoon brown sugar
1/8 to 1/4 teaspoon Tabasco pepper
    sauce
1 tablespoon water
1/2 teaspoon vegetable oil

Toast almonds on ungreased baking sheet in preheated 350°F. oven 10 minutes without stirring. Remove pan from oven and cool almonds in pan on wire rack. *Reduce oven temperature to 250°F.* Combine teriyaki sauce, brown sugar, pepper sauce and water in narrow 1-quart saucepan. Bring to boil over medium-low heat. Stir in almonds and boil about 5 minutes, or until sauce is absorbed by almonds, stirring frequently. Add oil and toss almonds until coated; turn out onto baking sheet, separating almonds. Bake 5 minutes; stir and turn almonds over. Bake 5 minutes longer. Remove almonds from pan to large plate; cool in single layer. Store in loose-fitting container or plastic bag.

EGG FLOWER SOUP WITH CORN

Makes about 4 1/2 cups

1 can (10 1/2 oz.) condensed
    chicken broth
2 soup cans water
2 slices fresh ginger root, each
    1/4 inch thick
2 tablespoons plus 2 teaspoons
    cornstarch
1/4 cup water
1/2 cup whole kernel corn
1 egg, beaten
2 tablespoons chopped green
    onions and tops
4 teaspoons Kikkoman Soy
    Sauce

Combine chicken broth, 2 soup cans water and ginger in medium saucepan. Bring to boil over high heat; reduce heat, cover and simmer 5 minutes. Discard ginger. Combine cornstarch and 1/4 cup water; stir into saucepan with corn. Cook over high heat, stirring constantly, until mixture boils and is slightly thickened. Gradually pour egg into boiling soup, stirring constantly, but gently, in 1 direction. Remove from heat; stir in green onions and soy sauce. Serve immediately.

BEEF

CLASSIC CHINESE PEPPER STEAK

Makes 4 servings

1 pound boneless beef sirloin steak
1 tablespoon Kikkoman Stir-Fry Sauce
2 tablespoons vegetable oil, divided
2 medium-size green, red or yellow bell peppers,
    cut into 1-inch squares
2 medium onions, cut into 1-inch squares
1/4 cup Kikkoman Stir-Fry Sauce
    Hot cooked rice (optional)

Cut beef across grain into thin strips, then into 1-inch squares; coat with 1 tablespoon stir-fry sauce. Heat 1 tablespoon oil in hot wok or large skillet over high heat. Add beef and stir-fry 1 minute; remove. Heat remaining 1 tablespoon oil in same pan. Add peppers and onions; stir-fry 5 minutes. Stir in beef and 1/4 cup stir-fry sauce; cook and stir just until beef and vegetables are coated with sauce. Serve immediately with rice.

牛肉食譜

SZECHUAN BEEF &
SNOW PEAS

Makes 2 to 3 servings

1/2 pound boneless tender beef
　　steak (sirloin, rib eye or
　　top loin)
2 tablespoons cornstarch,
　　divided
3 tablespoons Kikkoman Soy
　　Sauce, divided
1 tablespoon dry sherry
1 clove garlic, minced
3/4 cup water
1/4 to 1/2 teaspoon crushed red
　　pepper
2 tablespoons vegetable oil,
　　divided
6 ounces fresh snow peas,
　　trimmed
1 medium onion, chunked
　　Salt
1 medium tomato, chunked
　　Hot cooked rice

Slice beef across grain into thin strips.
Combine 1 tablespoon *each* cornstarch and soy sauce with sherry and
garlic in small bowl; stir in beef. Let
stand 15 minutes. Meanwhile, combine water, remaining 1 tablespoon
cornstarch, 2 tablespoons soy sauce
and red pepper; set aside. Heat 1 tablespoon oil in hot wok or large skillet
over high heat. Add beef and stir-fry 1
minute; remove. Heat remaining 1 tablespoon oil in same pan. Add snow
peas and onion; lightly sprinkle with
salt and stir-fry 3 minutes. Add beef,
soy sauce mixture and tomato. Cook
and stir until sauce boils and thickens
and tomato is heated through. Serve
immediately with rice.

DRAGON BEEF
KABOBS

Makes 4 servings

1 1/4 pounds boneless beef sirloin
　　steak, 1 1/2 inches thick
1/4 cup Kikkoman Teriyaki Sauce
1 tablespoon peanut butter
1 teaspoon brown sugar
1 teaspoon garlic powder
1/2 teaspoon Tabasco pepper
　　sauce
1 can (8 1/4 oz.) pineapple
　　chunks, drained

MICROWAVE DIRECTIONS:
Cut beef into 1 1/2-inch cubes; place
in medium bowl. Blend teriyaki
sauce, peanut butter, brown sugar,
garlic powder and pepper sauce.
Pour mixture over beef, turning
pieces over to coat thoroughly. Marinate 1 hour, turning pieces over occasionally. Reserving marinade,
remove beef and thread alternately
with pineapple chunks on 4 wooden
or bamboo skewers. Arrange skewers in single layer on 12-inch round
microwave-safe platter. Brush with
reserved marinade. Microwave on
High 2 minutes. Turn skewers over
and rotate positions on platter, mov-
ing center skewers to edge. Brush
with marinade. Microwave on High 2
minutes longer, or to desired degree
of doneness.

Szechuan Beef & Snow Peas

BEEF & NAPA WITH NOODLES

Makes 4 servings

- 1 small head napa (Chinese cabbage)
  Boiling water
- 1/2 pound boneless tender beef steak (sirloin, rib eye or top loin)
- 6 tablespoons Kikkoman Stir-Fry Sauce, divided
- 1/8 to 1/4 teaspoon crushed red pepper
- 2 tablespoons vegetable oil, divided
- 1/4 pound green onions, cut into 2-inch lengths, separating whites from tops
- 1 large red bell pepper, cut into strips
  Hot cooked vermicelli or thin spaghetti

Separate and rinse napa; pat dry. Thinly slice enough leaves crosswise to measure 8 cups; place in colander or large strainer. Pour boiling water over cabbage just until leaves wilt. Cool under cold water; drain thoroughly. Cut beef across grain into thin slices, then into strips. Combine 1 tablespoon stir-fry sauce and crushed red pepper in small bowl; stir in beef to coat. Heat 1 tablespoon oil in hot wok or large skillet over high heat. Add beef and stir-fry 1 minute; remove. Heat remaining 1 tablespoon oil in same pan; add white parts of green onions and stir-fry 1 minute. Add red bell pepper; stir-fry 2 minutes. Add green onion tops; stir-fry 2 minutes longer. Add beef, cabbage and remaining 5 tablespoons stir-fry sauce; cook and stir until vegetables are coated with sauce. Serve immediately over vermicelli.

Beef & Napa with Noodles

FIERY BEEF STIR-FRY

Makes 2 to 3 servings

/2 pound boneless tender beef
    steak (sirloin, rib eye or
    top loin)
1 tablespoon cornstarch
4 tablespoons Kikkoman Soy
    Sauce, divided
/2 teaspoon sugar
1 clove garlic, minced
/4 cups water
4 teaspoons cornstarch
/2 teaspoons distilled white
    vinegar
/8 to 1/4 teaspoon ground red
    pepper (cayenne)
3 tablespoons vegetable oil,
    divided
3 cups bite-size cauliflowerets
    Salt
1 onion, chunked and separated
1 green pepper, chunked

it beef across grain into thin strips.
ombine 1 tablespoon *each* corn-
arch and soy sauce with sugar and
rlic in small bowl; stir in beef. Let
and 15 minutes. Meanwhile, com-
ne water, remaining 3 tablespoons
y sauce, 4 teaspoons cornstarch,
negar and red pepper; set aside.
eat 1 tablespoon oil in hot wok or
rge skillet over high heat. Add beef
d stir-fry 1 minute; remove. Heat re-
aining 2 tablespoons oil in same
n. Add cauliflowerets; lightly sprin-
e with salt and stir-fry 2 minutes.
ld onion and green pepper; stir-fry
minutes. Stir in beef and soy sauce
xture; cook and stir until sauce
ils and thickens.

SZECHUAN BEEF STEW

Makes 6 servings

2 pounds boneless beef chuck
2 cloves garlic, pressed
4 tablespoons Kikkoman Soy
    Sauce, divided
3 teaspoons sugar, divided
1 cup water
1/2 to 3/4 teaspoon crushed red
    pepper
3/4 teaspoon fennel seed, crushed
1/4 teaspoon black pepper
1/4 teaspoon ground cloves
1/4 teaspoon ground ginger
1 tablespoon vegetable oil
2 tablespoons cornstarch
2 tablespoons water

Cut beef into 2-inch cubes. Combine
garlic, 2 tablespoons soy sauce and 1
teaspoon sugar in large bowl; stir in
beef cubes until well coated. Let stand
15 minutes. Meanwhile, combine 1
cup water, remaining 2 tablespoons
soy sauce, 2 teaspoons sugar, red pepper, fennel, black pepper, cloves and
ginger; set aside. Heat oil in Dutch
oven or large skillet over high heat.
Brown beef on all sides in hot oil. Stir
in soy sauce mixture. Bring to boil; reduce heat and simmer, covered, 2
hours, or until beef is very tender.
Combine cornstarch with 2 tablespoons water; stir into beef mixture.
Cook and stir until mixture boils and
thickens, about 1 minute.

GINGER BEEF WITH BOK CHOY

Makes 4 servings

- 3/4 **pound boneless tender beef steak (sirloin, rib eye or top loin)**
- 3 **tablespoons Kikkoman Lite Soy Sauce, divided**
- 1 **tablespoon cornstarch**
- 1 **tablespoon dry sherry**
- 1 **teaspoon minced fresh ginger root**
- 1 **clove garlic, minced**
- 3/4 **cup water**
- 2 **teaspoons cornstarch**
- 1/2 **pound bok choy cabbage or romaine lettuce**
- 2 **tablespoons vegetable oil, divided**
- 1 **medium onion, cut into 1/2-inch strips**
- 1 **tablespoon slivered fresh ginger root**

Cut beef across grain into thin slices. Combine 1 tablespoon *each* lite soy sauce, cornstarch and sherry with minced ginger and garlic in medium bowl; stir in beef. Let stand 30 minutes. Meanwhile, combine water, 2 teaspoons cornstarch and remaining 2 tablespoons lite soy sauce; set aside. Separate and rinse bok choy; pat dry. Cut leaves crosswise into 1-inch strips, separating stems from leaves. Heat 1 tablespoon oil in hot wok or large skillet over high heat. Add beef and stir-fry 1 minute; remove. Heat remaining 1 tablespoon oil in same pan. Add onion and slivered ginger; stir-fry 2 minutes. Add bok choy stems; stir-fry 1 minute. Add leaves; stir-fry 1 minute longer. Add beef and soy sauce mixture; cook and stir until sauce boils and thickens. Serve immediately.

Ginger Beef with Bok Choy

Beef with Leafy Greens

BEEF WITH LEAFY GREENS

Makes 2 to 3 servings

3/4 pound romaine lettuce
1/2 pound boneless tender beef
   steak (sirloin, rib eye or
   top loin)
4 tablespoons Kikkoman Stir-Fry
   Sauce, divided
1 clove garlic, minced
2 tablespoons vegetable oil,
   divided
1 medium onion, chunked
1 teaspoon minced fresh ginger
   root
8 cherry tomatoes, halved *or* 1
   medium tomato, chunked
2 tablespoons chopped unsalted
   peanuts

Separate and rinse lettuce; pat dry. Cut leaves crosswise into 1-inch strips; set aside. Cut beef across grain into thin slices. Combine 1 tablespoon stir-fry sauce and garlic in small bowl; stir in beef to coat. Heat 1 tablespoon oil in hot wok or large skillet over high heat. Add beef and stir-fry 1 minute; remove. Heat remaining 1 tablespoon oil in same pan. Add onion and ginger; stir-fry 2 minutes. Add lettuce; stir-fry 2 minutes longer. Add beef, tomatoes and remaining 3 tablespoons stir-fry sauce; cook and stir until vegetables are coated with sauce and tomatoes are just heated through. Serve immediately with peanuts.

SZECHUAN BEEF STIR-FRY

Makes 4 servings

1 pound boneless tender beef
  steak (sirloin, rib eye or
  top loin)
2 tablespoons cornstarch
3 tablespoons Kikkoman Soy
  Sauce, divided
1/2 teaspoon sugar
1/2 teaspoon crushed red pepper
1 large clove garlic, minced
2/3 cup water
1 1/2 teaspoons cornstarch
3 tablespoons vegetable oil,
  divided
1/4 pound green onions and tops,
  cut into 1 1/2-inch lengths,
  separating whites from tops

Cut beef across grain into thin slices, then into strips. Combine 2 tablespoons *each* cornstarch and soy sauce with sugar, red pepper and garlic in medium bowl; stir in beef. Let stand 20 minutes. Meanwhile, combine water, remaining 1 tablespoon soy sauce and 1 1/2 teaspoons cornstarch; set aside. Heat 2 tablespoons oil in hot wok or large skillet over high heat. Add beef and stir-fry 1 minute; remove. Heat remaining 1 tablespoon oil in same pan; add white parts of green onions and stir-fry 1 minute. Stir in beef, soy sauce mixture and green onion tops. Cook and stir until mixture boils and thickens. Serve immediately.

BEEF WITH SNOW PEAS & CAULIFLOWER

Makes 2 to 3 servings

1/2 pound boneless tender beef
  steak (sirloin, rib eye or
  top loin)
2 tablespoons cornstarch,
  divided
3 tablespoons Kikkoman Soy
  Sauce, divided
1/2 teaspoon sugar
1 clove garlic, minced
1 cup water, divided
1/4 to 1/2 teaspoon crushed red
  pepper
3 tablespoons vegetable oil,
  divided
1/2 pound fresh snow peas,
  trimmed
1 small head cauliflower,
  separated into flowerets
2 medium tomatoes, chunked
  Hot cooked rice

Cut beef across grain into thin slices. Combine 1 tablespoon *each* cornstarch and soy sauce with sugar and garlic in small bowl; stir in beef. Let stand 15 minutes. Meanwhile, combine 1/2 cup water, remaining 1 tablespoon cornstarch and 2 tablespoons soy sauce with red pepper; set aside. Heat 1 tablespoon oil in hot wok or large skillet over high heat. Add beef and stir-fry 1 minute; remove. Heat 1 tablespoon oil in same pan. Add snow peas and stir-fry 2 minutes; remove. Heat remaining 1 tablespoon oil in same pan; add cauliflowerets and stir-fry 2 minutes. Add remaining 1/2 cup water; cover and steam 3 minutes. Stir in beef, snow peas, tomatoes and soy sauce mixture. Cook and stir until mixture boils and thickens. Serve immediately with rice.

BEEF & TOMATO STIR-FRY SALAD

Makes 4 to 6 servings

- 1 pound boneless tender beef steak (sirloin, rib eye or top loin)
- 1 tablespoon cornstarch
- 4 tablespoons Kikkoman Soy Sauce, divided
- 1/2 teaspoon sugar
- 1 clove garlic, pressed
- 2 tablespoons water
- 1 tablespoon red wine vinegar
- 1 tablespoon tomato catsup
- 3 tablespoons vegetable oil, divided
- 1 teaspoon onion powder
- 4 cups shredded iceberg lettuce
- 2 stalks celery, cut diagonally into thin slices
- 1 green pepper, cut into julienne strips
- 2 teaspoons minced fresh ginger root
- 15 cherry tomatoes, halved

Beef & Tomato Stir-Fry Salad

Cut beef across grain into thin strips. Combine cornstarch, 2 tablespoons soy sauce, sugar and garlic in medium bowl; stir in beef. Let stand 15 minutes. Meanwhile, combine remaining 2 tablespoons soy sauce, water, vinegar, catsup, 1 tablespoon oil and onion powder; set aside. Line large shallow bowl or large platter with lettuce. Heat 1 tablespoon oil in hot wok or large skillet over high heat. Add beef and stir-fry 1 minute; remove. Heat remaining 1 tablespoon oil in same pan. Add celery, green pepper and ginger; stir-fry 1 minute. Remove pan from heat; stir in tomatoes, beef and soy sauce mixture. Spoon mixture over lettuce; toss well to combine before serving. Serve immediately.

SIMPLY SUPER SUKIYAKI

Makes 4 to 6 servings

1 block tofu
1/2 cup Kikkoman Soy Sauce
1/2 cup water
2 tablespoons sugar
3/4 pound ground beef
1 medium-size yellow onion, thinly sliced
1 pound fresh spinach, trimmed, washed and drained
1 bunch green onions and tops, cut into 2-inch lengths, separating whites from tops
1/4 pound fresh mushrooms, sliced

Cut tofu into 1-inch cubes; drain well on several layers of paper towels. Meanwhile, combine soy sauce, water and sugar; set aside. Brown beef in Dutch oven or large skillet over medium heat, stirring to break beef into large chunks. Add yellow onion; cook 1 minute. Add spinach, white parts of green onions, mushrooms and soy sauce mixture; cook until spinach wilts, stirring constantly. Gently stir in tofu and green onion tops. Cook 5 to 7 minutes, or until vegetables are tender and tofu is seasoned with sauce.

Simply Super Sukiyaki

MONGOLIAN BEEF

Makes 4 servings

3/4 pound boneless tender beef steak (sirloin, rib eye or top loin)
3 tablespoons cornstarch, divided
4 tablespoons Kikkoman Teriyaki Sauce, divided
1 tablespoon dry sherry
1 clove garlic, minced
1 cup water
1 teaspoon distilled white vinegar
1/4 to 1/2 teaspoon crushed red pepper
2 tablespoons vegetable oil, divided
2 carrots, cut diagonally into thin slices
1 onion, chunked and separated
1 green pepper, chunked

Cut beef across grain into strips, then into 1 1/2-inch squares. Combine 2 tablespoons cornstarch, 1 tablespoon teriyaki sauce, sherry and garlic in medium bowl; stir in beef. Let stand 30 minutes. Meanwhile, combine water, remaining 1 tablespoon cornstarch, 3 tablespoons teriyaki sauce, vinegar and red pepper; set aside. Heat 1 tablespoon oil in hot wok or large skillet over high heat. Add beef and stir-fry 1 minute; remove. Heat remaining 1 tablespoon oil in same pan. Add carrots, onion and green pepper; stir-fry 4 minutes. Add beef and teriyaki sauce mixture; cook and stir until sauce boils and thickens.

STIR-FRIED BEEF & EGGPLANT SALAD

Makes 2 to 3 servings

1/2 pound boneless tender beef steak (sirloin, rib eye or top loin)
1/3 cup Kikkoman Stir-Fry Sauce
1 teaspoon distilled white vinegar
1/4 to 1/2 teaspoon crushed red pepper
1 clove garlic, pressed
Lettuce leaves (optional)
3 cups finely shredded iceberg lettuce
3 tablespoons vegetable oil, divided
1 medium eggplant, cut into julienne strips
1 medium carrot, cut into julienne strips
6 green onions, cut into 1 1/2-inch lengths, separating whites from tops

Cut beef across grain into thin slices, then into strips. Combine stir-fry sauce, vinegar, red pepper and garlic. Coat beef with 1 tablespoon of the stir-fry sauce mixture; set aside remaining mixture. Line edge of large shallow bowl or large platter with lettuce leaves; arrange shredded lettuce in center. Heat 1 tablespoon oil in hot wok or large skillet over high heat. Add beef and stir-fry 1 minute; remove. Heat remaining 2 tablespoons oil in same pan; add eggplant and stir-fry 6 minutes. Add carrot and white parts of green onions; stir-fry 3 minutes. Add green onion tops; stir-fry 2 minutes longer. Add remaining stir-fry sauce mixture and beef. Cook and stir just until beef and vegetables are coated with sauce. Spoon mixture over shredded lettuce; toss well to combine before serving. Serve immediately.

BROCCOLI & BEEF STIR-FRY

Makes 2 to 3 servings

1/2 pound boneless tender beef steak (sirloin, rib eye or top loin)
1 tablespoon cornstarch
4 tablespoons Kikkoman Soy Sauce, divided
1 teaspoon sugar
1 teaspoon minced fresh ginger root
1 clove garlic, minced
1 pound fresh broccoli
1 1/4 cups water
4 teaspoons cornstarch
3 tablespoons vegetable oil, divided
1 onion, chunked
Hot cooked rice

Cut beef across grain into thin slices. Combine 1 tablespoon *each* cornstarch and soy sauce with sugar, ginger and garlic in small bowl; stir in beef. Let stand 15 minutes. Meanwhile, remove flowerets from broccoli; cut in half lengthwise. Peel stalks; cut crosswise into 1/8-inch slices. Combine water, 4 teaspoons cornstarch and remaining 3 tablespoons soy sauce; set aside. Heat 1 tablespoon oil in hot wok or large skillet over high heat. Add beef and stir-fry 1 minute; remove. Heat remaining 2 tablespoons oil in same pan. Add broccoli and onion; stir-fry 4 minutes. Stir in beef and soy sauce mixture. Cook and stir until mixture boils and thickens. Serve immediately over rice.

RED-COOKED SHORT RIBS

Makes 4 servings

- **3 pounds beef short ribs**
- **1/3 to 1/2 cup all-purpose flour**
- **2 tablespoons vegetable oil**
- **3/4 cups water, divided**
- **1/2 cup Kikkoman Teriyaki Sauce**
- **1 clove garlic, pressed**
- **1/2 teaspoon ground ginger**
- **1/8 teaspoon ground cloves**

Coat ribs thoroughly with flour; reserve 1/4 cup excess flour. Heat oil in Dutch oven or large saucepan over medium heat. Add ribs and brown slowly on all sides; drain off excess oil. Combine 1 1/4 cups water, teriyaki sauce, garlic, ginger and cloves; pour over ribs. Cover; simmer 2 hours, or until ribs are tender. Meanwhile, blend reserved flour and remaining 1/2 cup water. Remove ribs to serving platter; keep warm. Pour pan drippings into large measuring cup; skim off fat. Add enough water to measure 2 1/2 cups; return to pan and bring to boil. Gradually stir in flour mixture. Cook and stir until thickened; serve with ribs.

Red-Cooked Short Ribs

RED-COOKED BEEF & CARROTS

Makes 4 servings

- 1 pound boneless beef chuck
- 5 tablespoons Kikkoman Teriyaki Sauce, divided
- 1 large clove garlic, minced
- 1 tablespoon vegetable oil
- 3½ cups water, divided
- ½ teaspoon fennel seed, crushed
- ¼ teaspoon pepper
- ⅛ teaspoon ground cloves
- 3 carrots, cut into 1-inch lengths
- 3 green onions and tops, cut into 1-inch lengths, separating whites from tops
- 3 tablespoons cornstarch
  Hot cooked noodles

Cut beef into 1-inch cubes. Combine 2 tablespoons teriyaki sauce and garlic in medium bowl; stir in beef cubes and let stand 10 minutes. Heat oil in Dutch oven or large skillet over high heat. Add beef; stir-fry until lightly browned on all sides. Add 3 cups water, remaining 3 tablespoons teriyaki sauce, fennel, pepper and cloves; bring to boil. Reduce heat; cover and simmer 40 minutes. Add carrots and white parts of green onions. Simmer, covered, 20 minutes, or until beef and vegetables are tender. Meanwhile, mix cornstarch with remaining ½ cup water. Stir into beef mixture with green onion tops; cook and stir until mixture boils and thickens. Serve over noodles.

Red-Cooked Beef & Carrots

CANTONESE STIR-FRY

Makes 4 servings

3/4 **pound boneless beef sirloin,
     lean pork or chicken**
  1 **tablespoon Kikkoman Stir-Fry
     Sauce**
  2 **tablespoons vegetable oil,
     divided**
  2 **small zucchini, cut crosswise
     into 1/4-inch-thick slices**
  1 **onion, chunked**
 12 **cherry tomatoes, halved**
1/4 **cup Kikkoman Stir-Fry Sauce**

Cut beef, pork or chicken across grain into thin slices, then into slivers; coat with 1 tablespoon stir-fry sauce. Heat 1 tablespoon oil in hot wok or large skillet over high heat. Add beef and stir-fry 1 minute (stir-fry pork or chicken 2 minutes); remove. Heat remaining 1 tablespoon oil in same pan. Add zucchini and onion; stir-fry 4 minutes. Stir in beef, tomatoes and 1/4 cup stir-fry sauce. Cook and stir until beef and vegetables are coated with sauce and tomatoes are heated through. Serve immediately.

KOREAN RIBS

Makes 4 servings

  4 **pounds beef short ribs,
     2 1/2 inches long**
2/3 **cup Kikkoman Teriyaki Sauce**
  1 **tablespoon sesame seed,
     toasted**
  1 **teaspoon sugar**
  2 **teaspoons Tabasco pepper
     sauce**
  2 **large cloves garlic, pressed**

Score meaty side of ribs, opposite bone, 1/2 inch apart, 1/2 inch deep, lengthwise and crosswise. Place ribs in large plastic bag. Combine teriyaki sauce, sesame seed, sugar, pepper sauce and garlic; pour over ribs. Press air out of bag; tie top securely. Refrigerate 4 hours, turning bag over occasionally. Remove ribs and broil or grill 4 inches from heat source or hot coals 15 to 18 minutes, or until outsides of ribs are brown and crisp. Turn ribs over occasionally during cooking.

STUFFED TERIYAKI STEAKS

Makes 6 to 8 servings

  2 **boneless beef sirloin steaks,
     each cut 1/2 inch thick
     (about 1 pound each)**
1/2 **cup Kikkoman Teriyaki Sauce**
  6 **green onions and tops
     Boiling water**

Pound each steak evenly to 1/4-inch thickness. Spread steaks out in large pan; pour in teriyaki sauce and turn steaks over to thoroughly coat each piece. Marinate 15 minutes, turning steaks over occasionally. Meanwhile, place green onions in shallow pan. Pour enough boiling water over onions to cover; drain immediately and cool. Remove steaks from marinade; spread out flat. Place 3 green onions lengthwise in center of each steak. Roll steaks up lengthwise, jelly-roll fashion, around onions; secure with string or wooden picks. Broil or grill 4 to 6 inches from heat source or hot coals 10 to 12 minutes (for rare), or to desired doneness, turning rolls over frequently. To serve, cut rolls crosswise into 3-inch pieces; remove string or picks.

ORIENTAL PORK BUNDLES

Makes 4 to 6 servings

Plum Sauce (recipe follows)
1/3 cup Kikkoman Stir-Fry Sauce
1 clove garlic, pressed
1/2 pound boneless lean pork, diced
1/2 teaspoon vegetable oil
2 eggs, beaten
2 tablespoons vegetable oil, divided
2 stalks celery, diced
1 medium carrot, diced
1 small onion, diced
2 ounces fresh mushrooms, coarsely chopped
6 (8-inch) flour tortillas, warmed
3 cups finely shredded iceberg lettuce

Prepare Plum Sauce on page 42; cool while preparing filling. Combine stir-fry sauce and garlic. Coat pork with 1 tablespoon stir-fry sauce mixture; let stand 10 minutes. Meanwhile, heat 1/2 teaspoon oil in hot wok or large skillet over medium-high heat. Pour in eggs and scramble; remove. Heat 1 tablespoon oil in same pan. Add pork and stir-fry 3 minutes; remove. Heat remaining 1 tablespoon oil in same pan. Add celery, carrot, onion and mushrooms; stir-fry 4 minutes. Stir in eggs, pork and remaining stir-fry sauce mixture. Cook and stir just until pork and vegetables are coated with sauce. Spread 1 tablespoon Plum Sauce on each tortilla; top with desired amount of shredded lettuce and pork mixture. Wrap or fold over to enclose filling.

豬肉食譜

PLUM SAUCE:

Combine ¼ cup plum jam, 2 table-spoons Kikkoman Stir-Fry Sauce and ½ teaspoon distilled white vinegar in small saucepan. Cook, stirring constantly, over medium-high heat until mixture comes to a boil and is smooth.

CASHEW PORK STIR-FRY

Makes 4 servings

- ¾ pound boneless lean pork
- 1 tablespoon Kikkoman Stir-Fry Sauce
- 3 tablespoons vegetable oil, divided
- 2 stalks celery, cut diagonally into ½-inch slices
- 1 onion, chunked
- 1 large green pepper, chunked
- ¼ pound fresh mushrooms, sliced
- 2 medium tomatoes, chunked
- ¼ cup Kikkoman Stir-Fry Sauce
- ¼ cup roasted cashews

Cut pork across grain into thin slices; coat with 1 tablespoon stir-fry sauce. Heat 1 tablespoon oil in hot wok or large skillet over medium-high heat. Add pork and stir-fry 3 minutes; remove. Wipe out pan with paper towel. Heat remaining 2 tablespoons oil in same pan over high heat. Add celery, onion and green pepper; stir-fry 2 minutes. Add mushrooms and stir-fry 2 minutes longer. Add pork, tomatoes and ¼ cup stir-fry sauce. Cook and stir only until tomatoes are heated through. Just before serving, sprinkle cashews over pork and vegetables.

HAWAIIAN PORK STEW

Makes 6 servings

- 2 pounds boneless pork shoulder (Boston butt)
- ¼ cup all-purpose flour
- 1 teaspoon ground ginger
- 2 tablespoons vegetable oil
- 1 can (8 oz.) pineapple chunks in juice
- 1¾ cups water, divided
- ⅓ cup Kikkoman Teriyaki Sauce
- 1 pound fresh yams or sweet potatoes, peeled and cut into 2-inch chunks
- 1 large onion, cut into eighths
  Hot cooked rice

Cut pork into 1½-inch cubes. Coat in mixture of flour and ginger; reserve 2 tablespoons flour mixture. Heat oil in Dutch oven or large pan; brown pork on all sides in hot oil. Drain pineapple; reserve juice. Add juice, 1 cup water and teriyaki sauce to pork. Cover pan; bring to boil. Reduce heat and simmer 1 hour, stirring occasionally. Add yams to pork; simmer, covered 10 minutes. Stir in onion; simmer, covered, 20 minutes longer, or until pork and yams are tender. Meanwhile, combine reserved flour mixture and remaining ¾ cup water; stir into pork mixture and cook until slightly thickened. Stir in pineapple; cook only until heated through. Serve with rice.

HUNAN PORK STIR-FRY

Makes 2 to 3 servings

½ **pound boneless lean pork**
2 **teaspoons cornstarch**
6 **teaspoons Kikkoman Lite Soy Sauce, divided**
2 **cloves garlic, minced and divided**
¾ **cup water**
1 **tablespoon cornstarch**
⅛ **to ¼ teaspoon crushed red pepper**
3 **tablespoons vegetable oil, divided**
3 **cups bite-size cauliflowerets**
1 **medium-size green pepper, chunked**
2 **medium tomatoes, cut into eighths**
Hot cooked rice

Cut pork across grain into thin slices, then into strips. Combine 2 teaspoons *each* cornstarch and lite soy sauce with ½ of the garlic in small bowl; stir in pork. Let stand 30 minutes. Meanwhile, combine water, 1 tablespoon cornstarch, remaining 4 teaspoons lite soy sauce and red pepper; set aside. Heat 1 tablespoon oil in hot wok or large skillet over high heat. Add pork and stir-fry 2 minutes; remove. Heat remaining 2 tablespoons oil in same pan over medium-high heat. Add cauliflowerets and remaining garlic; stir-fry 2 minutes. Add green pepper; stir-fry 3 minutes. Stir in tomatoes, pork and soy sauce mixture. Cook and stir gently until sauce boils and thickens. Serve with rice.

Hunan Pork Stir-Fry

Tofu & Vegetable Stir-Fry

TOFU & VEGETABLE STIR-FRY

Makes 4 servings

1/2 block tofu
1 pound napa (Chinese cabbage) or romaine lettuce*
1/2 cup water
2 tablespoons cornstarch, divided
4 tablespoons Kikkoman Soy Sauce, divided
1/4 pound boneless lean pork
2 teaspoons minced fresh ginger root
1 clove garlic, minced
1/2 teaspoon sugar
2 tablespoons vegetable oil, divided
1 medium onion, chunked
2 medium tomatoes, chunked

Cut tofu into 1/2-inch cubes; drain well on several layers of paper towels. Separate and rinse cabbage; pat dry. Cut leaves crosswise into 1-inch strips; set aside. Blend water, 1 tablespoon cornstarch and 3 tablespoons soy sauce; set aside. Cut pork into thin slices, then into thin strips. Combine remaining 1 tablespoon cornstarch and 1 tablespoon soy sauce, ginger, garlic and sugar in small bowl; stir in pork. Heat 1 tablespoon oil in hot wok or large skillet over high heat. Add pork and stir-fry 2 minutes; remove. Heat remaining 1 tablespoon oil in same pan. Add onion; stir-fry 2 minutes. Add cabbage; stir-fry 1 minute. Add tomatoes, pork and soy sauce mixture. Cook and stir gently until sauce boils and thickens. Gently fold in tofu; heat through.

*If using romaine, increase water to 2/3 cup.

PORK & VEGETABLES OVER CRUSTY NOODLE CAKE

Makes 4 to 6 servings

1/2 pound boneless lean pork
3 tablespoons cornstarch, divided
4 tablespoons Kikkoman Soy Sauce, divided
1 clove garlic, minced
1 can (14 oz.) chicken broth
Crusty Noodle Cake (recipe follows)
2 tablespoons vegetable oil, divided
1 teaspoon minced fresh ginger root
2 stalks celery, cut diagonally into thin slices
2 large carrots, cut into julienne strips
1 onion, thinly sliced
1/2 pound fresh bean sprouts

Cut pork across grain into thin slices, then into strips. Combine 1 tablespoon *each* cornstarch and soy sauce with garlic in small bowl. Stir in pork until coated; set aside. Combine remaining 2 tablespoons cornstarch, 3 tablespoons soy sauce and chicken broth; set aside. Prepare Crusty Noodle Cake. Heat 1 tablespoon oil in same skillet over high heat. Add pork and stir-fry 2 minutes; remove. Heat remaining 1 tablespoon oil in same skillet; add ginger and stir-fry 15 seconds. Add celery, carrots and onion; stir-fry 2 minutes. Add bean sprouts and stir-fry 2 minutes longer. Stir in pork and soy sauce mixture. Cook and stir until mixture boils and thickens, about 1 minute. Spoon over noodle cake and serve immediately.

CRUSTY NOODLE CAKE:

Cook *8 ounces vermicelli* according to package directions. Drain; rinse under cold water and drain thoroughly. Heat *1 tablespoon vegetable oil* in large, nonstick skillet over medium-high heat. Add vermicelli all at once; slightly spread to fill bottom of skillet to form noodle cake. Without stirring, cook 6 minutes, or until golden on bottom. Lift cake with wide spatula; add *1 tablespoon oil* to skillet. Turn cake over. Cook 6 minutes longer, or until golden brown, shaking skillet occasionally to brown evenly; remove to serving platter and keep warm.

HAWAIIAN ROAST PORK

Makes 6 servings

1 (3-pound) boneless pork shoulder roast (Boston butt)
1/2 cup Kikkoman Soy Sauce
1 1/2 teaspoons liquid smoke seasoning

Cut pork in half lengthwise. Place halves in large plastic bag. Combine soy sauce and liquid smoke; pour over pork. Press air out of bag; tie top securely. Turn over several times to coat pieces well. Refrigerate 8 hours or overnight, turning bag over occasionally. Remove pork from marinade and place in shallow baking pan; cover with aluminum foil. Bake at 350°F. 30 minutes. Discard foil; turn pieces over. Bake 1 hour longer, or until meat thermometer inserted into thickest part registers 170°F. To serve, cut across grain into thin slices.

CHINESE
TEA-SMOKED RIBS

Makes 3 to 4 servings

16 bags or 6 tablespoons loose
    black tea leaves
1½ teaspoons fennel seed,
    crushed
½ teaspoon ground ginger
½ teaspoon ground cloves
½ teaspoon black pepper
    Nonstick cooking spray
3 pounds pork spareribs, sawed
    into thirds across bones
½ cup Kikkoman Teriyaki Baste
    & Glaze
1 tablespoon tomato catsup
1 clove garlic, minced
⅛ teaspoon ground red pepper
    (cayenne)

Remove tea leaves from bags; com
bine with fennel, ginger, cloves an
black pepper. Thoroughly spray larg
rack and large shallow baking pa
with cooking spray. Sprinkle tea mi
ture evenly in pan. Cut ribs into 1-ri
pieces and place, meaty side up, o
rack over tea mixture. Cover pan wit
foil and bake at 350°F. 30 minute
Meanwhile, combine teriyaki baste &
glaze, catsup, garlic and red peppe
set aside. Remove ribs from oven; *r
duce oven temperature to 325°F. R*
serving about 2 tablespoonfuls, brus
both sides of ribs with baste & glaz
mixture; return to oven and bake, ur
covered, 40 minutes. Brush tops o
ribs with reserved baste & glaze mi
ture; bake 5 minutes longer. Garnis
as desired.

Chinese Tea-Smoked Ribs

IMPERIAL STIR-FRY

Makes 2 to 3 servings

1/2 pound boneless lean pork
2 tablespoons cornstarch,
   divided
4 tablespoons Kikkoman Teriyaki
   Sauce, divided
1 teaspoon minced fresh ginger
   root
1 clove garlic, minced
1 cup water
1 tablespoon dry sherry
1/8 teaspoon salt
2 tablespoons vegetable oil,
   divided
1 large carrot, cut into julienne
   strips
2 stalks celery, cut diagonally
   into 1/4-inch slices
1 medium onion, chunked and
   separated
1 medium-size green pepper, cut
   into 1/4-inch strips

Cut pork across grain into thin slices, then into narrow strips. Blend 1 tablespoon *each* cornstarch and teriyaki sauce with ginger and garlic in small bowl; stir in pork. Let stand 30 minutes. Meanwhile, combine water, remaining 1 tablespoon cornstarch, 3 tablespoons teriyaki sauce, sherry and salt; set aside. Heat 1 tablespoon oil in hot wok or large skillet over high heat. Add pork and stir-fry 3 minutes; remove. Heat remaining 1 tablespoon oil in same pan; add carrot and stir-fry 1 minute. Add celery, onion and green pepper; stir-fry 2 minutes. Stir in pork and teriyaki sauce mixture. Cook and stir until sauce boils and thickens. Serve immediately.

SZECHUAN PORK SALAD

Makes 2 to 3 servings

1/2 pound boneless lean pork
4 tablespoons Kikkoman Teriyaki
   Sauce, divided
1/8 to 1/4 teaspoon crushed red
   pepper
1 cup water
2 tablespoons cornstarch
1 tablespoon distilled white
   vinegar
2 tablespoons vegetable oil,
   divided
1 onion, chunked and separated
12 radishes, thinly sliced
2 medium zucchini, cut into
   julienne strips
   Salt
4 cups shredded lettuce

Cut pork across grain into thin slices, then into narrow strips. Combine pork, 1 tablespoon teriyaki sauce and red pepper in small bowl; set aside. Combine water, cornstarch, remaining 3 tablespoons teriyaki sauce and vinegar; set aside. Heat 1 tablespoon oil in hot wok or large skillet over high heat. Add pork and stir-fry 2 minutes; remove. Heat remaining 1 tablespoon oil in same pan. Add onion; stir-fry 2 minutes. Add radishes and zucchini; lightly sprinkle with salt and stir-fry 1 minute longer. Stir in pork and teriyaki sauce mixture. Cook and stir until mixture boils and thickens. Spoon over bed of lettuce on serving platter; serve immediately.

GLAZED PORK TENDERLOIN

Makes 4 to 6 servings

2 pork tenderloins, about
  ¾ pound each
½ cup Kikkoman Teriyaki Baste
  & Glaze
¼ teaspoon anise seed, crushed
¼ teaspoon pepper
⅛ teaspoon ground cloves
  Mustard-Soy Dipping Sauce
  (recipe follows)

Place tenderloins on rack in shallow foil-lined baking pan; tuck under thin ends of each tenderloin. Combine teriyaki baste & glaze, anise, pepper and cloves; brush each tenderloin thoroughly with baste & glaze mixture. Bake in 325°F. oven 1 hour, or until meat thermometer inserted into thickest part registers 170°F. Brush occasionally with baste & glaze mixture during baking. Remove from oven and let stand 15 minutes. Cut across grain into thin slices and serve with Mustard-Soy Dipping Sauce.

MUSTARD-SOY DIPPING SAUCE:
Blend *2 tablespoons dry mustard* with *1 teaspoon each distilled white vinegar* and *water* to make a smooth paste. Cover and let stand 10 minutes. Thin with enough *Kikkoman Soy Sauce* to dipping consistency.

HUNAN STIR-FRY WITH TOFU

Makes 4 servings

1 block tofu
½ pound ground pork
1 tablespoon dry sherry
1 teaspoon minced fresh ginger
  root
1 clove garlic, minced
½ cup regular-strength chicken
  broth
1 tablespoon cornstarch
3 tablespoons Kikkoman Soy
  Sauce
1 tablespoon vinegar
½ teaspoon crushed red pepper
1 tablespoon vegetable oil
1 onion, cut into ¾-inch pieces
1 green pepper, cut into ¾-inch
  pieces
  Hot cooked rice

Cut tofu into ½-inch cubes; drain well on several layers of paper towel. Meanwhile, combine pork, sherry, ginger and garlic in small bowl; let stand 10 minutes. Blend broth, cornstarch, soy sauce, vinegar and red pepper; set aside. Heat wok or large skillet over medium-high heat; add pork. Cook, stirring to separate pork, about 3 minutes, or until lightly browned; remove. Heat oil in same pan. Add onion and green pepper; stir-fry 4 minutes. Add pork and soy sauce mixture. Cook and stir until mixture boils and thickens. Gently fold in tofu; heat through. Serve immediately over rice.

Hunan Stir-Fry with Tofu

COLORFUL STIR-FRIED PORK

Makes 4 servings

- ⅓ cup Kikkoman Stir-Fry Sauce
- 1 teaspoon distilled white vinegar
- ¼ to ½ teaspoon crushed red pepper
- ¾ pound boneless lean pork
- 1 tablespoon Kikkoman Stir-Fry Sauce
- 3 tablespoons vegetable oil, divided
- 2 medium carrots, cut into julienne strips
- 1 medium onion, halved and sliced
- ¼ pound fresh snow peas, trimmed and cut lengthwise in half

Combine ⅓ cup stir-fry sauce, vinegar and red pepper; set aside. Cut pork across grain into thin slices, then into strips; coat with 1 tablespoon stir-fry sauce. Heat 1 tablespoon oil in hot wok or large skillet over high heat. Add pork and stir-fry 2 minutes; remove. Heat remaining 2 tablespoons oil in same pan. Add carrots, onion and snow peas; stir-fry 4 minutes. Stir in pork and stir-fry sauce mixture. Cook and stir just until pork and vegetables are coated with sauce. Serve immediately.

Colorful Stir-Fried Pork

CRISPY LITE SPARERIBS

Makes 4 to 6 servings

4 pounds pork spareribs, sawed into thirds across bones
¼ cup Kikkoman Lite Soy Sauce
2 tablespoons dry sherry
1 clove garlic, pressed
Mandarin Peach Sauce (recipe follows)

Cut ribs into 1-rib pieces. Place in steamer basket or on steamer rack. Set basket in large pot or wok of boiling water. (Do not allow water level to reach ribs.) Cover and steam 30 minutes. Meanwhile, combine lite soy sauce, sherry and garlic in large bowl; add ribs and stir to coat each piece well. Marinate 1 hour, stirring frequently. Remove ribs and place, meaty side up, on rack of broiler pan. Bake in 425°F. oven 15 minutes, or until crispy. Serve with warm Mandarin Peach Sauce.

MANDARIN PEACH SAUCE:

Drain *1 can (16 oz.) cling peach slices in juice or extra light syrup;* reserve liquid for another use. Place peaches in blender container. Process on high speed until smooth; pour into small saucepan. Combine *3 tablespoons Kikkoman Teriyaki Sauce* and *1 tablespoon cornstarch;* stir into peaches with *1 tablespoon sugar, ¼ teaspoon fennel seed, crushed, ¼ teaspoon pepper* and *⅛ teaspoon ground cloves.* Bring mixture to boil over medium heat. Simmer until sauce thickens, about 2 minutes, stirring constantly. Remove from heat and stir in *⅛ teaspoon garlic powder.* Makes 1 cup.

PORK CHOPS TERIYAKI

Makes 4 to 6 servings

1 can (8 oz.) pineapple chunks in juice
1 tablespoon vegetable oil
6 boneless pork chops, ¾ inch thick
½ cup Kikkoman Teriyaki Sauce
¼ cup water
1 clove garlic, minced
1 tablespoon sesame seed, toasted
2 teaspoons grated fresh ginger root
1 tablespoon cornstarch
1 tablespoon water
½ cup finely chopped green onions and tops

Drain pineapple; reserve juice. Heat oil in Dutch oven over medium-high heat. Brown pork chops on both sides in hot oil. Combine reserved juice, teriyaki sauce, ¼ cup water, garlic, sesame seed and ginger; pour over chops and simmer, covered, 30 minutes. Turn chops over and continue cooking, covered, 30 minutes longer, or until chops are tender; remove. Dissolve cornstarch in 1 tablespoon water and stir into pan juices. Cook and stir until sauce boils and thickens. Stir in pineapple chunks and green onions, cooking until pineapple is heated through. Return chops to pan and coat both sides with sauce.

BAKE & GLAZE TERI RIBS

Makes 4 servings

3 pounds pork spareribs
1/2 teaspoon garlic powder
1/2 teaspoon pepper
2/3 cup Kikkoman Teriyaki Baste & Glaze
1/2 teaspoon grated lemon peel

Cut ribs into serving pieces; place, meaty side up, in shallow foil-lined baking pan. Sprinkle garlic powder and pepper evenly over ribs; cover pan loosely with foil. Bake in 350°F. oven 45 minutes. Meanwhile, combine teriyaki baste & glaze and lemon peel. Remove foil and brush both sides of ribs with baste & glaze mixture. Cover and bake 40 minutes longer, or until ribs are tender, brushing with baste & glaze mixture occasionally.

GLAZED PORK ROAST

Makes 6 servings

1 (3-pound) boneless pork shoulder roast (Boston Butt)
1 cup Kikkoman Teriyaki Sauce
3 tablespoons brown sugar, packed
3 tablespoons dry sherry
1 teaspoon minced fresh ginger root
1 clove garlic, minced
1/4 cup water
2 tablespoons sugar
1 tablespoon cornstarch

MICROWAVE DIRECTIONS:
Pierce meaty parts of roast with fork; place in large plastic bag. Combine teriyaki sauce, brown sugar, sherry, ginger and garlic; pour over roast. Press air out of bag; tie top securely. Refrigerate 8 hours or overnight, turning bag over occasionally. Reserving marinade, remove roast and place, fat side down, in 8 × 8-inch shallow microwave-safe dish. Brush thoroughly with reserved marinade. Cover roast loosely with waxed paper. Microwave on Medium-high (70%) 30 minutes, or until meat thermometer inserted into thickest part registers 165°F., rotating dish once and brushing with marinade. Remove roast; let stand 10 minutes before slicing. Meanwhile, combine reserved marinade, water, sugar and cornstarch in 2-cup microwave-safe measuring cup. Microwave on High 3 minutes, until mixture boils and thickens, stirring occasionally. Serve teriyaki glaze with roast.

PORK AND PEANUT STIR-FRY

Makes 2 to 3 servings

- 1/4 pound boneless lean pork
- 4 teaspoons cornstarch, divided
- 3 tablespoons Kikkoman Lite Soy Sauce, divided
- 1 teaspoon minced fresh ginger root
- 1/2 cup water
- 2 teaspoons distilled white vinegar
- 1/4 teaspoon garlic powder
- 2 tablespoons vegetable oil, divided
- 1 medium onion, sliced
- 1 medium carrot, cut diagonally into 1/8-inch-thick slices
- 2 medium zucchini, cut diagonally into 1/8-inch-thick slices
- 1/3 cup unsalted roasted peanuts
  Hot cooked rice (optional)

Cut pork across grain into thin slices, then into strips. Combine 2 teaspoons *each* cornstarch and lite soy sauce with ginger in small bowl; stir in pork. Let stand 15 minutes. Meanwhile, combine water, remaining 2 teaspoons cornstarch, 2 tablespoons plus 1 teaspoon lite soy sauce, vinegar and garlic powder; set aside. Heat 1 tablespoon oil in hot wok or large skillet over high heat. Add pork and stir-fry 2 minutes; remove. Heat remaining 1 tablespoon oil in same pan. Add onion and carrot; stir-fry 2 minutes. Add zucchini; stir-fry 2 minutes. Stir in pork and soy sauce mixture. Cook and stir until mixture boils and thickens. Stir in peanuts; serve immediately with rice.

Pork and Peanut Stir-Fry

POULTRY

SPICY CHICKEN

Makes 4 servings

3/4 pound boneless chicken
3 tablespoons Kikkoman Soy Sauce, divided
1 tablespoon cornstarch
1 tablespoon dry sherry
4 teaspoons water
2 tablespoons vegetable oil
1 teaspoon minced fresh ginger root
3/4 teaspoon crushed red pepper
1 small onion, chunked
1 small red or green bell pepper, cut into matchsticks
1 small zucchini, cut into matchsticks
1/2 cup water

Cut chicken into thin slices. Combine chicken and 1 tablespoon soy sauce in small bowl; let stand 30 minutes. Meanwhile, combine remaining 2 tablespoons soy sauce, cornstarch, sherry and 4 teaspoons water. Heat oil in hot wok or large skillet over high heat. Add ginger and crushed red pepper; cook until fragrant. Add chicken and stir-fry 3 minutes. Add onion, bell pepper, zucchini and 1/2 cup water; mix well. Cover and cook 1 minute, or until vegetables are tender-crisp. Add soy sauce mixture; cook and stir until sauce boils and thickens.

禽類食譜

MANDARIN CHICKEN SALAD

Makes 4 servings

- 1 whole chicken breast, split
- 2 cups water
- 4 tablespoons Kikkoman Soy Sauce, divided
  Boiling water
- 3/4 pound fresh bean sprouts
- 1 carrot, peeled and shredded
- 1/2 cup slivered green onions and tops
- 2 tablespoons minced fresh cilantro or parsley
- 1/4 cup distilled white vinegar
- 2 teaspoons sugar
- 1/2 cup blanched slivered almonds, toasted

Simmer chicken in mixture of 2 cups water and 1 tablespoon soy sauce in covered saucepan 15 minutes, or until chicken is tender. Meanwhile, pour boiling water over bean sprouts. Drain; cool under cold water and drain thoroughly. Remove chicken and cool. (Refrigerate stock for another use, if desired.) Skin and bone chicken; shred meat with fingers into large mixing bowl. Add bean sprouts, carrot, green onions and cilantro. Blend vinegar, sugar and remaining 3 tablespoons soy sauce, stirring until sugar dissolves. Pour over chicken and vegetables; toss to coat all ingredients. Cover and refrigerate 1 hour. Just before serving, add almonds and toss to combine.

SPICY SMOKED DUCK

Makes 4 servings

1 (4- to 5-pound) frozen
   duckling, thawed
¹/₄ cup Kikkoman Lite Soy Sauce
1 teaspoon liquid smoke
   seasoning
¹/₂ teaspoon fennel seed, well
   crushed
¹/₄ teaspoon pepper
¹/₈ teaspoon ground cloves

Remove and discard giblets and neck from duckling cavity. Wash duckling; drain and gently pat dry with paper towels. Combine lite soy sauce, liquid smoke, fennel, pepper and cloves. Brush body cavity with sauce mixture. Place duckling, breast side up, on rack in roasting pan. Roast at 425°F. 1 hour. *Reduce oven temperature to 350°F.* Continue roasting 45 minutes, or until tender. Brush skin of duckling several times with sauce mixture during last 30 minutes of cooking time. Let stand 15 minutes before carving.

Spicy Smoked Duck

SHANGHAI TURKEY STIR-FRY

Makes 6 servings

1 small turkey thigh, skinned
   and boned
3 tablespoons cornstarch,
   divided
4 tablespoons Kikkoman Soy
   Sauce, divided
1 tablespoon dry sherry
1 tablespoon minced fresh
   ginger root
1 clove garlic, minced
1 cup water
3 tablespoons vegetable oil,
   divided
1 large carrot, cut into julienne
   strips
1 onion, sliced
1 package (10 oz.) frozen
   French-style green beans,
   thawed and drained

Cut turkey into thin, narrow strips; set aside. Combine 2 tablespoons *each* cornstarch and soy sauce with sherry, ginger and garlic in medium bowl; stir in turkey. Let stand 30 minutes. Meanwhile, combine water, remaining 1 tablespoon cornstarch and 2 tablespoons soy sauce; set aside. Heat 2 tablespoons oil in hot wok or large skillet over high heat. Add turkey and stir-fry 3 minutes, or until tender; remove. Heat remaining 1 tablespoon oil in same pan. Add carrot and onion; stir-fry 2 minutes. Add green beans; stir-fry 1 minute longer. Stir in turkey and soy sauce mixture. Cook and stir until mixture boils and thickens. Serve immediately.

CHICKEN WITH BOK CHOY

Makes 2 to 3 servings

1/2 chicken breast, skinned and boned
2 tablespoons cornstarch, divided
4 tablespoons Kikkoman Teriyaki Sauce, divided
1 tablespoon minced fresh ginger root
3/4 cup water
1 pound bok choy cabbage or romaine lettuce
3 tablespoons vegetable oil, divided
1 onion, chunked and separated
1/2 pound fresh mushrooms, sliced
1 clove garlic, minced

Cut chicken into narrow strips. Combine 1 tablespoon *each* cornstarch and teriyaki sauce with ginger in small bowl; stir in chicken. Let stand 10 minutes. Meanwhile, combine water, the remaining 1 tablespoon cornstarch and 3 tablespoons teriyaki sauce; set aside. Separate and rinse bok choy; pat dry. Cut leaves crosswise into 2-inch strips, separating stems from leaves. Heat 1 tablespoon oil in hot wok or large skillet over high heat. Add chicken and stir-fry 1 minute; remove. Heat remaining 2 tablespoons oil in same pan. Add bok choy stems, onion, mushrooms and garlic; stir-fry 4 minutes. Add bok choy leaves; stir-fry 1 minute. Add chicken and teriyaki sauce mixture; cook and stir until sauce thickens and boils.

KUNG PAO STIR-FRY

Makes 4 servings

1 whole chicken breast, skinned and boned
2 tablespoons cornstarch, divided
3 tablespoons Kikkoman Teriyaki Sauce, divided
1/4 teaspoon ground red pepper (cayenne)
3/4 cup water
4 teaspoons distilled white vinegar
3/4 pound romaine lettuce
2 tablespoons vegetable oil, divided
1/3 cup roasted peanuts

Cut chicken into thin strips. Combine 1 tablespoon *each* cornstarch and teriyaki sauce with red pepper in small bowl; stir in chicken. Let stand 15 minutes. Meanwhile, combine water, remaining 1 tablespoon cornstarch and 2 tablespoons teriyaki sauce with vinegar; set aside. Separate and rinse lettuce; pat dry. Cut leaves crosswise into 2-inch strips. Heat 1 tablespoon oil in hot wok or large skillet over high heat. Add chicken and stir-fry 2 minutes; remove. Heat remaining 1 tablespoon oil in same pan. Add lettuce; stir-fry 1 minute. Stir in chicken and teriyaki sauce mixture. Cook and stir until mixture boils and thickens. Remove from heat; stir in peanuts. Serve immediately.

SHANTUNG CHICKEN

Makes 4 servings

1 whole chicken breast, skinned
   and boned
2 tablespoons cornstarch,
   divided
3 tablespoons Kikkoman Soy
   Sauce, divided
1 tablespoon dry sherry
1 clove garlic, minced
1 cup water
3 tablespoons vegetable oil,
   divided
1/2 pound fresh bean sprouts
1/4 pound green onions and tops,
   cut into 1 1/2-inch lengths,
   separating whites from tops
1 tablespoon slivered fresh
   ginger root
1 tablespoon sesame seed,
   toasted
   Hot cooked noodles

Cut chicken into narrow strips. Combine 1 tablespoon *each* cornstarch and soy sauce with sherry and garlic in small bowl; stir in chicken. Let stand 5 minutes. Meanwhile, blend water, remaining 1 tablespoon cornstarch and 2 tablespoons soy sauce; set aside. Heat 1 tablespoon oil in hot wok or large skillet over high heat. Add chicken and stir-fry 2 minutes; remove. Heat remaining 2 tablespoons oil in same pan; add bean sprouts, white parts of green onions and ginger; stir-fry 3 minutes. Stir in chicken, soy sauce mixture, green onion tops and sesame seed. Cook and stir until mixture boils and thickens. Serve immediately over noodles.

Shantung Chicken

BRAISED CHINESE DUCKLING

Makes 4 servings

1 (4- to 5-pound) frozen
    duckling, thawed and
    quartered
3 tablespoons Kikkoman Lite
    Soy Sauce, divided
1 tablespoon vegetable oil
2 tablespoons dry sherry
1 clove garlic, minced
1 teaspoon ginger juice*
4 green onions and tops, cut into
    2-inch lengths
1/3 cup water
2 teaspoons cornstarch

Wash duckling quarters; dry with paper towels. Rub thoroughly with 2 tablespoons lite soy sauce. Let stand 30 minutes. Heat oil in Dutch oven or large skillet over medium heat. Brown duckling slowly in hot oil; drain off fat. Add sherry and garlic. Cover and cook over low heat 45 minutes, or until tender, turning quarters over once. Remove from pan; keep warm. Spoon off and discard excess fat from pan juices; return 1/3 cup juices to pan. Add remaining 1 tablespoon lite soy sauce, ginger juice and green onions; cook 1 minute. Combine water with cornstarch; stir into pan. Cook and stir until sauce boils and thickens. To serve, spoon sauce over duckling quarters.

*Peel fresh ginger root, then squeeze through garlic press.

GOLDEN CHICKEN STIR-FRY

Makes 4 servings

1 whole chicken breast, skinned
    and boned
1 tablespoon cornstarch
5 tablespoons Kikkoman Teriyaki
    Sauce, divided
1 clove garlic, minced
1 1/4 cups regular-strength chicken
    broth
4 teaspoons cornstarch
    Boiling water
1/2 pound fresh bean sprouts
2 cups finely shredded lettuce
2 tablespoons vegetable oil,
    divided
2 medium carrots, cut into
    julienne strips
1 onion, chunked
2 teaspoons slivered fresh ginger
    root

Cut chicken into thin strips. Combine 1 tablespoon *each* cornstarch and teriyaki sauce with garlic in small bowl; stir in chicken. Let stand 15 minutes. Meanwhile, combine chicken broth, remaining 4 tablespoons teriyaki sauce and 4 teaspoons cornstarch; set aside. Pour boiling water over bean sprouts in bowl; let stand 1 minute. Drain; rinse under cold water and drain thoroughly. Toss sprouts with lettuce. Line serving platter with mixture; set aside. Heat 1 tablespoon oil in hot wok or large skillet over high heat. Add chicken and stir-fry 2 minutes; remove. Heat remaining 1 tablespoon oil in same pan. Add carrots, onion and ginger; stir-fry 4 minutes. Add chicken and teriyaki sauce mixture. Cook and stir until sauce boils and thickens. Turn out onto lined platter; toss to combine before serving.

Golden Chicken Stir-Fry

CHINESE-STYLE POT ROAST CHICKEN

Makes 4 servings

3 pounds frying chicken pieces
1/4 cup Kikkoman Soy Sauce
2 tablespoons vegetable oil
1 tablespoon dry sherry
1 clove garlic, minced
2 stalks celery, cut diagonally
    into 1/4-inch slices
2 green onions and tops, cut into
    1-inch lengths
3/4 cup water
1 tablespoon cornstarch
2 tablespoons Kikkoman Soy
    Sauce
1 teaspoon sugar

Rinse chicken pieces and pat dry with paper towels. Rub chicken thoroughly with 1/4 cup soy sauce; let stand 15 minutes. Heat oil in Dutch oven or large skillet over medium heat; add chicken and brown slowly in hot oil. Add sherry and garlic; cover and simmer 30 minutes, or until tender. Remove chicken from pan; keep warm. Add celery and green onions to pan; cook 1 to 2 minutes. Combine water, cornstarch, 2 tablespoons soy sauce and sugar; stir into pan and cook until thickened. Serve sauce and vegetables over chicken.

JADE & RUBY STIR-FRY

Makes 4 servings

1 whole chicken breast, skinned
    and boned
1 pound fresh broccoli
2 tablespoons vegetable oil
1 medium onion, chunked
2 tablespoons water
2 medium-size red bell peppers,
    chunked
1/2 pound fresh mushrooms,
    quartered
1/3 cup Kikkoman Stir-Fry Sauce
1/4 teaspoon crushed red pepper

Cut chicken into 1-inch square pieces. Remove flowerets from broccoli; cut into bite-size pieces. Peel stalks; cut into thin slices. Heat oil in hot wok or large skillet over high heat. Add chicken; stir-fry 1 minute. Add broccoli and onion; stir-fry 1 minute. Add water; cover and cook 2 minutes, stirring once. Add bell peppers and mushrooms; stir-fry 2 minutes. Stir in stir-fry sauce and crushed red pepper. Cook and stir until chicken and vegetables are coated with sauce. Serve immediately.

Chinese-Style Pot Roast Chicken

THAI HENS

Makes 4 to 6 servings

3 fresh or thawed Rock Cornish
    hens (1¼ to 1½ pounds
    each)
½ cup Kikkoman Teriyaki Sauce
1 tablespoon grated lemon peel
1 tablespoon lemon juice
2 cloves garlic, pressed
¼ to ½ teaspoon ground red
    pepper (cayenne)
1 tablespoon minced fresh
    cilantro

Remove and discard giblets and necks
from hens. Split hens lengthwise.
Rinse halves under cold running water; drain well and pat dry with paper
towels. Place in large plastic bag.
Combine teriyaki sauce, lemon peel
and juice, garlic and red pepper; pour
over hens. Press air out of bag; tie top
securely. Turn bag over several times
to coat halves. Refrigerate 8 hours or
overnight, turning bag over occasionally. Reserving marinade, remove
hens and place on rack of broiler pan.
Broil about 7 inches from heat source
45 to 50 minutes, or until tender, turning over frequently and brushing with
reserved marinade. Remove to serving
platter and immediately sprinkle ci-
antro over hens.

LOTUS CHICKEN
CHOP SUEY

Makes 2 to 3 servings

½ chicken breast, skinned and
    boned
4 tablespoons Kikkoman Teriyaki
    Sauce, divided
1 cup water
2 tablespoons cornstarch
1 tablespoon dry sherry
1 large carrot, cut diagonally
    into ⅛-inch slices
1 onion, chunked and separated
⅛ teaspoon salt
¼ pound fresh bean sprouts
1 package (6 oz.) frozen Chinese
    pea pods, thawed and
    drained

MICROWAVE DIRECTIONS:
Cut chicken into narrow strips; place
in small bowl. Stir in 2 tablespoons
teriyaki sauce; let stand 20 minutes.
Meanwhile, blend water, cornstarch,
sherry and remaining 2 tablespoons
teriyaki sauce in 2-cup microwave-safe
measuring cup. Microwave on High 4
minutes, until mixture boils and thickens, stirring occasionally to prevent
lumping; set aside. Combine carrot,
onion and salt in 2-quart microwave-
safe casserole. Microwave, covered, on
High 4 minutes, stirring after 2 minutes. Stir in bean sprouts; cover and
microwave on High 1 minute. Stir in
chicken; microwave, covered, on High
3 minutes, stirring once. Combine
cornstarch mixture with chicken and
vegetables. Microwave, uncovered, on
High 1 minute. Stir in pea pods. Microwave, uncovered, on High 2 minutes, or until mixture is heated
through, stirring once.

COLORFUL DRAGON STIR-FRY

Makes 4 servings

1 whole chicken breast, skinned
  and boned
1 pound fresh broccoli
5 tablespoons Kikkoman Stir-Fry
  Sauce, divided
3 tablespoons vegetable oil,
  divided
1 medium onion, cut into thin
  wedges
1 medium carrot, cut diagonally
  into thin slices
2 tablespoons water

Cut chicken into 1/2-inch strips. Remove flowerets from broccoli; set aside. Peel stalks; cut into thin slices. Coat chicken with 1 tablespoon stir-fry sauce. Heat 1 tablespoon oil in hot wok or large skillet over high heat. Add chicken and stir-fry 3 minutes; remove. Heat remaining 2 tablespoons oil in same pan. Add onion; stir-fry 1 minute. Add broccoli and carrot; stir-fry 2 minutes longer. Pour water into pan. Reduce heat and simmer, covered, 3 minutes; stir once. Add remaining 4 tablespoons stir-fry sauce and chicken. Cook and stir just until chicken and vegetables are coated. Serve immediately.

Colorful Dragon Stir-Fry

LETTUCE-WRAPPED PLUM CHICKEN

Makes 8 servings

Orange-Plum Sauce (recipe follows)
1 whole chicken breast, skinned and boned
3 tablespoons Kikkoman Soy Sauce, divided
4 teaspoons cornstarch, divided
1/4 cup water
2 tablespoons vegetable oil, divided
1/2 cup diced carrots
1 cup diced celery
1/2 cup diced onion
1 tablespoon minced fresh ginger root
8 large iceberg lettuce leaves

Prepare Orange-Plum Sauce; cool to room temperature. Meanwhile, dice chicken breast. Combine 1 tablespoon soy sauce and 3 teaspoons cornstarch in small bowl; stir in chicken. Let stand 10 minutes. Combine the remaining 2 tablespoons soy sauce, 1 teaspoon cornstarch and water; set aside. Heat 1 tablespoon oil in hot wok or large skillet over high heat. Add chicken and stir-fry 2 minutes; remove. Heat remaining 1 tablespoon oil in same pan. Add carrots and stir-fry 1 minute. Add celery, onion and ginger; stir-fry 2 minutes longer. Stir in chicken and soy sauce mixture. Cook and stir until mixture boils and thickens. To serve, spread about 2 teaspoons Orange-Plum Sauce in center of each lettuce leaf. Fill each leaf with about 1/4 cup chicken mixture; fold lettuce around filling to enclose.

ORANGE-PLUM SAUCE:

Blend 1/2 cup plum jam, 1/2 teaspoon grated fresh orange peel, 1 pressed garlic clove, 2 tablespoons Kikkoman Teriyaki Sauce, 2 tablespoons orange juice and 1 teaspoon cornstarch in small saucepan. Bring to boil over medium-high heat; reduce heat and simmer 1 minute, stirring constantly.

CHICKEN ADOBO

Makes 4 servings

3 pounds frying chicken pieces
1/2 cup Kikkoman Soy Sauce
1/2 cup distilled white vinegar
2 tablespoons sugar
1 teaspoon pepper
6 large cloves garlic, pressed

MICROWAVE DIRECTIONS:
Rinse chicken pieces and pat dry with paper towels. Combine soy sauce, vinegar, sugar, pepper and garlic in large microwave-safe casserole with lid; add chicken pieces, skin side down. Cover and microwave on High 10 minutes. Turn chicken pieces over; rearrange in dish. Cover and microwave on High 13 minutes longer, or until chicken is tender, rearranging pieces once. Serve immediately.

ORIENTAL TURKEY TERRINE

Makes 6 to 8 servings

2 1/2 pounds ground turkey
  2 eggs, beaten
  3/4 cup finely chopped onion
  1/4 cup chopped fresh cilantro
      or parsley
  1/4 cup Kikkoman Soy Sauce
1 1/2 cups dry bread crumbs
  1/2 teaspoon ground ginger
  1/4 teaspoon fennel seed, crushed
  1/4 teaspoon pepper
  1/8 teaspoon ground cloves
      Dash ground cinnamon

Combine turkey, eggs, onion, cilantro and soy sauce in large bowl; set aside. Stir together bread crumbs, ginger, fennel, pepper, cloves and cinnamon. Sprinkle evenly over turkey mixture, mixing until thoroughly blended. Press firmly into greased 12-cup Bundt or tube pan. Bake at 375°F. 45 minutes, or until top is lightly browned and starts to pull away from side of pan. Turn out onto serving platter; let stand 5 minutes before cutting into thin slices.

NOTE: If desired, press turkey mixture into greased 9 1/4 × 5 1/4-inch loaf pan; bake at 375°F. 1 hour, or to doneness described above.

ORANGE-CASHEW CHICKEN

Makes 4 servings

  1 pound boneless chicken
      breasts
  1/2 cup Kikkoman Teriyaki Baste
      & Glaze
  2 tablespoons orange juice
  2 tablespoons dry white wine
  2 tablespoons vegetable oil
  1 green pepper, cut into thin
      strips
  1/2 cup diagonally sliced celery
  1 can (11 oz.) mandarin orange
      segments, drained
  1/2 cup roasted cashews

Cut chicken into thin slices. Combine teriyaki baste & glaze, orange juice and wine; set aside. Heat oil in hot wok or large skillet over medium heat. Add chicken, green pepper and celery; stir-fry 3 to 4 minutes. Pour in baste & glaze mixture; cook and stir until chicken and vegetables are coated with sauce. Remove from heat; stir in orange segments and cashews. Serve immediately.

Chicken Teriyaki Kabobs

CHICKEN TERIYAKI KABOBS

Makes 4 servings

- ¹/₂ pounds chicken breasts, skinned and boned
- 1 bunch green onions, cut into 1-inch lengths
- ¹/₂ cup Kikkoman Soy Sauce
- 2 tablespoons sugar
- 1 teaspoon vegetable oil
- 1 teaspoon minced fresh ginger root
- 1 clove garlic, minced

Cut chicken into 1¹/₂-inch square pieces. Thread each of eight 6-inch bamboo or metal skewers alternately with chicken and green onion pieces. (Spear green onion pieces through side.) Place skewers in shallow pan. Combine soy sauce, sugar, oil, ginger and garlic; pour over skewers and brush chicken thoroughly with sauce. Marinate 30 minutes. Reserving marinade, remove skewers and place on rack of broiler pan. Broil 3 minutes; turn over and brush with reserved marinade. Broil 3 minutes longer, or until chicken is tender.

SPICY CASHEW STIR-FRY

Makes 4 servings

- 3 chicken breast halves, skinned and boned
- 2 tablespoons vegetable oil
- 2 teaspoons minced fresh ginger root
- 6 to 8 whole red chili peppers
- 1 small onion, thinly sliced
- 1 small zucchini, thinly sliced
- 2 tablespoons chicken broth or water
- 1 tablespoon dry sherry
- 3 tablespoons Kikkoman Stir-Fry Sauce
- ¹/₂ cup unsalted roasted cashews

Cut chicken into thin slices. Place wok or large skillet over high heat until hot. Add oil, swirling to coat sides of pan. Add ginger and chili peppers; cook and stir until fragrant. Add chicken and stir-fry 3 minutes. Add onion, zucchini, broth, sherry and stir-fry sauce; cover and cook 1 minute, or until vegetables are tender-crisp. Stir in cashews; serve immediately.

HEARTY CHICKEN STIR-FRY WITH NOODLES

Makes 4 servings

- 1 whole chicken breast, skinned and boned
- 1 tablespoon cornstarch
- 5 tablespoons Kikkoman Teriyaki Sauce, divided
- 1 clove garlic, minced
- 1 cup water
- 4 teaspoons cornstarch
- 2 teaspoons tomato catsup
- 2 medium zucchini
- 2 cups uncooked fine egg noodles
- 2 tablespoons vegetable oil, divided
- 1 medium onion, chunked
- 10 cherry tomatoes, halved

Cut chicken into ½-inch square pieces. Combine 1 tablespoon *each* cornstarch and teriyaki sauce with garlic in small bowl; stir in chicken. Let stand 30 minutes. Meanwhile, combine water, remaining 4 tablespoons teriyaki sauce, 4 teaspoons cornstarch and catsup; set aside. Cut zucchini in half lengthwise, then diagonally into 1-inch pieces. Cook noodles according to package directions; drain and keep warm on serving plate. Heat 1 tablespoon oil in hot wok or large skillet over high heat. Add chicken and stir-fry 2 minutes; remove. Heat remaining 1 tablespoon oil in same pan. Add zucchini and onion; stir-fry 4 minutes. Add chicken, teriyaki sauce mixture and tomatoes. Cook and stir until sauce boils and thickens. Pour over noodles; toss to combine before serving.

Hearty Chicken Stir-Fry with Noodles

SZECHUAN DRAGON STIR-FRY

Makes 4 servings

1 whole chicken breast, skinned and boned
1 tablespoon cornstarch
4 tablespoons Kikkoman Soy Sauce, divided
1/2 teaspoon sugar
1 clove garlic, minced
1 cup water
4 teaspoons cornstarch
1/4 to 1/2 teaspoon crushed red pepper
2 tablespoons vegetable oil, divided
2 carrots, cut diagonally into thin slices
1 onion, chunked
2 small zucchini, cut in half lengthwise, then diagonally chunked
1/4 cup unsalted peanuts
Hot cooked rice

Cut chicken into thin, narrow strips. Combine 1 tablespoon *each* cornstarch and soy sauce with sugar and garlic in small bowl; stir in chicken and set aside. Blend water, 4 teaspoons cornstarch, remaining 3 tablespoons soy sauce and red pepper; set aside. Heat 1 tablespoon oil in hot wok or large skillet over high heat. Add chicken and stir-fry 2 minutes; remove. Heat remaining 1 tablespoon oil in same pan. Add carrots and onion; stir-fry 3 minutes. Add zucchini; stir-fry 2 minutes. Add chicken and soy sauce mixture. Cook and stir until sauce boils and thickens. Just before serving, stir in peanuts. Serve immediately with rice.

BEIJING CHICKEN

Makes 4 servings

3 pounds frying chicken pieces
1/2 cup Kikkoman Teriyaki Sauce
1 tablespoon dry sherry
2 teaspoons minced fresh ginger root
1/2 teaspoon fennel seed, crushed
1/2 teaspoon grated orange peel
1/2 teaspoon honey

Rinse chicken pieces and pat dry with paper towels; place in large plastic bag. Combine teriyaki sauce, sherry, ginger, fennel, orange peel and honey; pour over chicken. Press air out of bag; tie top securely. Refrigerate 8 hours or overnight, turning bag over occasionally. Reserving marinade, remove chicken and place on rack of broiler pan. Broil 5 to 7 inches from heat source about 40 minutes, or until chicken is tender, turning pieces over and basting occasionally with reserved marinade.

MONGOLIAN POT

Makes 4 to 6 servings

2 whole chicken breasts, skinned
and boned
4 tablespoons Kikkoman Soy
Sauce, divided
2 teaspoons minced fresh ginger
root
1/2 teaspoon sugar
2 cans (10 1/4 oz. each)
condensed chicken broth
4 soup cans water
1 large clove garlic, minced
1/2 pound cabbage, cut into
3/4-inch chunks (about
4 cups)
3/4 pound fresh spinach, trimmed,
washed and drained
3 green onions and tops, cut into
1-inch lengths and slivered
4 ounces vermicelli or thin
spaghetti, cooked and
drained
1/4 pound fresh mushrooms,
sliced

Cut chicken into thin strips. Combine
2 tablespoons soy sauce, ginger and
sugar in medium dish; stir in chicken.
Let stand 15 minutes. Meanwhile,
combine chicken broth, water, remaining 2 tablespoons soy sauce and
garlic in deep electric skillet or electric wok; bring to boil. Reduce heat;
keep broth mixture hot. Arrange cabbage, spinach, green onions, vermicelli and mushrooms on platter. Using
chopsticks or tongs, let individuals se-
lect and add chicken, vegetables and
vermicelli to hot broth. Cook chicken
until tender, vegetables to desired
doneness and vermicelli until heated
through. Serve in individual bowls
with additional soy sauce, as desired.
When all foods are cooked, serve
broth as soup.

GINGER CHICKEN
STIR-FRY

Makes 4 servings

1 whole chicken breast, skinned
and boned
4 tablespoons Kikkoman Teriyaki
Sauce, divided
3 teaspoons minced fresh ginger
root, divided
1 cup water
2 tablespoons cornstarch
2 tablespoons vegetable oil,
divided
2 carrots, cut into julienne strips
1 medium onion, sliced
3/4 pound fresh spinach, washed,
drained and torn in half

Cut chicken into thin strips. Combine
chicken, 1 tablespoon teriyaki sauce
and 2 teaspoons ginger in small bowl;
let stand 10 minutes. Meanwhile,
combine water, cornstarch, remaining
3 tablespoons teriyaki sauce and 1
teaspoon ginger; set aside. Heat 1 tablespoon oil in hot wok or large skillet
over high heat. Add chicken and stir-
fry 2 minutes; remove. Heat remaining 1 tablespoon oil in same pan. Add
carrots and onion; stir-fry 2 minutes.
Stir in chicken and teriyaki sauce mixture. Cook and stir until mixture boils
and thickens. Stir in spinach; serve
immediately.

Cantonese Chicken Salad

CANTONESE CHICKEN SALAD

Makes 6 servings

3 chicken breast halves
2 cups water
5 tablespoons Kikkoman Soy
    Sauce, divided
4 cups shredded iceberg lettuce
1 medium carrot, peeled and
    shredded
1/2 cup finely chopped green
    onions and tops
1/3 cup distilled white vinegar
2 tablespoons sesame seed,
    toasted
2 teaspoons sugar
1/2 teaspoon ground ginger
2 tablespoons minced fresh
    cilantro or parsley

Simmer chicken in mixture of water and 1 tablespoon soy sauce in covered saucepan 15 minutes, or until chicken is tender. Remove chicken and cool. (Refrigerate stock for another use, if desired.) Skin and bone chicken; shred meat with fingers into large mixing bowl. Add lettuce, carrot and green onions. Combine vinegar, remaining 4 tablespoons soy sauce, sesame seed, sugar and ginger; stir until sugar dissolves. Pour over chicken and vegetables; toss to coat all ingredients. Cover and refrigerate 1 hour. Just before serving, add cilantro and toss to combine. Garnish as desired.

SAUCY SHRIMP OVER CHINESE NOODLE CAKES

Makes 4 servings

Chinese Noodle Cakes (recipe follows)
1¼ cups water
  2 tablespoons cornstarch, divided
  4 tablespoons Kikkoman Soy Sauce, divided
  1 teaspoon tomato catsup
½ pound medium-size raw shrimp, peeled and deveined
  2 tablespoons vegetable oil, divided
  1 clove garlic, minced
½ teaspoon minced fresh ginger root
  1 green pepper, chunked
  1 medium onion, chunked
  2 stalks celery, cut diagonally into thin slices
  2 tomatoes, chunked

Prepare Chinese Noodle Cakes on page 74. Combine water, 1 tablespoon cornstarch and 3 tablespoons soy sauce with catsup; set aside. Blend remaining 1 tablespoon cornstarch and 1 tablespoon soy sauce in small bowl; stir in shrimp until coated. Heat 1 tablespoon oil in hot wok or large skillet over high heat. Add shrimp and stir-fry 1 minute; remove. Heat remaining 1 tablespoon oil in same pan. Add garlic and ginger; stir-fry until fragrant. Add green pepper, onion and celery; stir-fry 4 minutes. Stir in soy sauce mixture, shrimp and tomatoes. Cook and stir until sauce boils and thickens. Cut Chinese Noodle Cakes into squares and serve with shrimp mixture.

海鮮食譜

CHINESE NOODLE CAKES:

Cook *8 ounces capellini* (angel hair pasta) according to package directions. Drain; rinse under cold water and drain thoroughly. Heat *1 tablespoon vegetable oil* in large, non-stick skillet over medium-high heat. Add half the capellini; slightly spread to fill bottom of skillet to form noodle cake. Without stirring, cook 5 minutes, or until golden on bottom. Lift cake with wide spatula; add *1 tablespoon oil* to skillet and turn cake over. Cook 5 minutes longer, or until golden brown, shaking skillet occasionally to brown evenly; remove to rack and keep warm in 200°F. oven. Repeat with remaining capellini.

SZECHUAN SQUID STIR-FRY

Makes 4 servings

1 pound fresh or thawed medium
    squid
    Boiling water
2 tablespoons cornstarch,
    divided
4 tablespoons Kikkoman Teriyaki
    Sauce, divided
³/₄ cup water
¹/₈ to ¹/₄ teaspoon crushed red
    pepper
2 tablespoons vegetable oil,
    divided
1 red bell pepper, cut into
    ¹/₄-inch strips
¹/₄ pound green onions and tops,
    cut into 2-inch lengths,
    separating whites from tops
1 tablespoon minced fresh
    ginger root
1 clove garlic, minced
3 cups shredded iceberg lettuce

Clean, skin and wash squid.* Cut body sacs into ¹/₄-inch rings; place in bowl with tentacles. Add enough boiling water to cover; let stand 3 minutes. Drain; cool under cold water and drain thoroughly. Spread on paper towels and blot dry. Combine 1 table-spoon *each* cornstarch and teriyaki sauce in medium bowl; stir in squid. Let stand 10 minutes. Meanwhile combine water, remaining 1 table-spoon cornstarch, 3 tablespoons teri-yaki sauce and crushed red pepper; set aside. Heat 1 tablespoon oil in hot wok or large skillet over medium-high heat. Add squid and stir-fry 2 minutes; remove. Heat remaining 1 table-spoon oil in same pan. Add red bell pepper, white parts of green onions, ginger and garlic; stir-fry 2 minutes. Stir in squid, lettuce, green onion tops and teriyaki sauce mixture. Cook and stir until mixture boils and thickens. Serve immediately.

*To clean squid, carefully pull heads from body sacs; discard viscera. Set aside heads with tentacles. Remove transparent quill from inside sacs; wash insides thoroughly to remove all matter. Pull off speckled outer skin covering sacs. Cut tentacles from heads; discard hard "beaks" and heads.

SHANGHAI SHRIMP
STIR-FRY

Makes 4 servings

2 tablespoons cornstarch,
  divided
3 tablespoons Kikkoman Soy
  Sauce, divided
1 tablespoon minced fresh
  ginger root
/2 teaspoon sugar
/2 pound medium-size raw
  shrimp, peeled and deveined
/4 cups water
/4 teaspoon fennel seed, crushed
/8 teaspoon ground cloves
/8 teaspoon pepper
1 pound fresh broccoli
3 tablespoons vegetable oil,
  divided
1 onion, chunked and separated

ombine 1 tablespoon *each* corn-
arch and soy sauce with ginger and
gar in small bowl; stir in shrimp. Let
and 10 minutes. Meanwhile, com-
ne water, remaining 1 tablespoon
rnstarch and 2 tablespoons soy
uce, fennel, cloves and pepper; set
ide. Remove flowerets from broc-
li; cut into bite-size pieces. Peel
alks; cut into thin slices. Heat 1 ta-
espoon oil in hot wok or large skillet
er high heat. Add shrimp and stir-
/ 1 minute; remove. Heat remaining
tablespoons oil in same pan. Add
occoli; stir-fry 2 minutes. Add on-
n; stir-fry 3 minutes longer. Stir in
rimp and soy sauce mixture; cook
d stir until sauce boils and thickens.

CHINESE PORCUPINE
MEATBALLS

Makes 4 servings

^{1}/2 cup uncooked rice
 6 ounces medium-size raw
  shrimp
 1 pound ground pork
^{2}/3 cup chopped green onions
  and tops
 3 tablespoons Kikkoman Soy
  Sauce
 1 tablespoon dry sherry
 2 cloves garlic, pressed
  Mandarin Peach Sauce (see
  page 51)

Cover rice with warm water and let
stand 20 minutes; drain. Meanwhile,
peel, devein and mince shrimp. Combine shrimp with pork, green onions,
soy sauce, sherry, garlic and rice; mix
well. Divide into 8 equal portions;
shape portions into meatballs. Arrange meatballs on steamer rack. Set
rack in large saucepan or wok of boiling water. (Do not allow water level to
reach meatballs.) Cover and steam 45
minutes, or until meatballs are
cooked. Serve with warm Mandarin
Peach Sauce.

Chinese Porcupine Meatballs

TERIYAKI TROUT

Makes 4 servings

4 medium trout (about
  2 pounds), dressed
1/2 cup Kikkoman Teriyaki Sauce
1/4 teaspoon grated lemon peel
3 tablespoons lemon juice
4 teaspoons Kikkoman Teriyaki
  Sauce

Score both sides of trout with diagonal slashes 1/4 inch deep and 1 inch apart; place in large shallow pan. Pour 1/2 cup teriyaki sauce over trout, turning over to coat both sides well. Cover and refrigerate 1 hour, turning over once. Meanwhile, combine lemon peel and juice and 4 teaspoons teriyaki sauce; set aside. Reserving marinade, remove trout and place on rack of broiler pan. Broil 3 inches from heat source, 5 minutes on each side, or until fish flakes easily when tested with fork; brush occasionally with reserved marinade. Serve with lemon-teriyaki sauce.

SHRIMP & VEGETABLE STIR-FRY

Makes 4 servings

2 tablespoons cornstarch,
  divided
4 tablespoons Kikkoman Teriyaki
  Sauce, divided
1 tablespoon minced fresh
  ginger root
1/2 pound medium-size raw
  shrimp, peeled and deveined
3/4 cup water
2 tablespoons vegetable oil,
  divided
2 stalks celery, cut diagonally
  into 1/4-inch-thick slices
1 medium-size red bell pepper,
  cut into 1-inch squares
1/4 pound green onions and tops,
  cut into 1-inch lengths,
  separating whites from tops

Combine 1 tablespoon *each* cornstarch and teriyaki sauce with ginger in small bowl; add shrimp and stir to coat evenly. Let stand 15 minutes. Meanwhile, combine water, remaining 1 tablespoon cornstarch and 3 tablespoons teriyaki sauce; set aside. Heat 1 tablespoon oil in hot wok or large skillet over high heat. Add shrimp and stir-fry 1 minute; remove. Heat remaining 1 tablespoon oil in same pan. Add celery, red pepper and white parts of green onions; stir-fry 2 minutes. Stir in shrimp, teriyaki sauce mixture and green onion tops. Cook and stir until mixture boils and thickens. Serve over rice, if desired.

Teriyaki Trout

EMPEROR'S SWEET & SOUR FISH

Makes 4 to 6 servings

1¹/₂ **pounds fresh or thawed fish fillets, ¹/₂ inch thick**
 1 **can (6 oz.) unsweetened pineapple juice**
¹/₄ **cup Kikkoman Soy Sauce**
¹/₄ **cup water**
¹/₄ **cup sugar**
 2 **tablespoons cornstarch**
 3 **tablespoons vinegar**
 2 **tablespoons tomato catsup**
   Dash ground red pepper (cayenne)
¹/₄ **cup minced green onions and tops**

MICROWAVE DIRECTIONS:
Place fish in single layer in large microwave-safe dish; set aside. Combine pineapple juice, soy sauce, water, sugar, cornstarch, vinegar, catsup and red pepper in 2-cup microwave-safe measuring cup. Microwave on High 5 minutes, or until mixture boils and thickens, stirring occasionally to prevent lumping. Remove ¹/₄ cup sauce and pour over fillets, turning each piece over to coat both sides. Keep remaining sauce warm. Cover fish with waxed paper; microwave on High 8 minutes, or until fish flakes easily when tested with fork, turning dish once. Remove fillets to serving platter with slotted spoon. To serve, drizzle warm sauce over fillets and sprinkle green onions over sauce. Pass remaining sauce.

GINGER FISH FILLETS

Makes 4 servings

1 pound fresh or thawed fish
  fillets
1/4 cup Kikkoman Teriyaki Sauce
1 tablespoon vegetable oil
1 teaspoon sugar
1 tablespoon slivered fresh
  ginger root
1 large green onion and top, cut
  into 1-inch lengths and
  slivered
1/3 cup water
1 1/2 teaspoons cornstarch

Place fillets in single layer in shallow baking pan. Combine teriyaki sauce, oil and sugar; pour over fish. Turn fillets over to coat well. Marinate 20 minutes, turning fish over occasionally. (If fillets are very thin, marinate for only 10 minutes.) Sprinkle ginger and green onion evenly over each fillet. Bake in marinade at 350°F. 6 to 10 minutes, or until fish flakes easily when tested with fork. Remove to serving platter and keep warm; reserve 1/4 cup pan juices. Blend water and cornstarch in small saucepan. Stir in reserved pan juices. Cook and stir until mixture boils and thickens. To serve, spoon sauce over fish.

SEA BREEZE FISH SALAD

Makes 4 servings

1 pound firm white fish fillets
  (red snapper, sea bass or
  orange roughy), about 1 inch
  thick
1 3/4 cups water
1 tablespoon grated lemon peel
6 tablespoons lemon juice,
  divided
3 tablespoons Kikkoman Lite
  Soy Sauce, divided
6 ounces fresh snow peas,
  trimmed and cut diagonally
  into 1-inch pieces
2 tablespoons vegetable oil
1 tablespoon minced onion
1/2 teaspoon thyme, crumbled
1/4 teaspoon sugar
1/2 medium cantaloupe, chunked
1 tablespoon minced fresh
  cilantro or parsley

Cut fish into 1-inch cubes. Combine water, lemon peel, 4 tablespoons lemon juice and 1 tablespoon lite soy sauce in large skillet. Heat only until mixture starts to simmer. Add fish; simmer, uncovered, 3 minutes, or until fish flakes easily when tested with fork. Remove fish with slotted spoon to plate. Cool slightly; cover and refrigerate 1 hour, or until thoroughly chilled. Meanwhile, cook snow peas in boiling water 2 minutes, or until tender-crisp; cool under cold water and drain thoroughly. Chill. Measure remaining 2 tablespoons lemon juice and 2 tablespoons lite soy sauce, oil, onion, thyme and sugar into jar with screw-top lid; cover and shake well. Combine peas, cantaloupe and cilantro in large bowl; add dressing and toss to coat all ingredients. Add fish and gently stir to combine. Serve immediately.

Grilled Oriental Fish Steaks

GRILLED ORIENTAL FISH STEAKS

Makes 4 servings

4 fish steaks (halibut, salmon or swordfish), about ³/₄ inch thick
¹/₄ cup Kikkoman Lite Soy Sauce
3 tablespoons minced onion
1 tablespoon chopped fresh ginger root
1 tablespoon sesame seed, toasted
¹/₂ teaspoon sugar

Place fish in single layer in shallow baking pan. Measure lite soy sauce, onion, ginger, sesame seed and sugar into blender container; process on low speed 30 seconds, scraping sides down once. Pour sauce over fish; turn over to coat both sides. Marinate 30 minutes, turning fish over occasionally. Remove fish and broil or grill 4 inches from heat source or moderately hot coals 5 minutes on each side, or until fish flakes easily when tested with fork. Garnish as desired.

ORIENTAL STEAMED FISH

Makes 4 servings

4 white fish steaks, about ³/₄ inch thick
1 tablespoon slivered fresh ginger root
¹/₄ cup orange juice
2 tablespoons Kikkoman Soy Sauce
1¹/₂ teaspoons distilled white vinegar
¹/₂ teaspoon brown sugar
1 teaspoon Oriental sesame oil
2 green onions and tops, minced

Place fish, in single layer, on oiled rack of bamboo steamer; sprinkle ginger evenly over fish. Set rack in large pot or wok of boiling water. (Do not allow water level to reach fish.) Cover and steam 8 to 10 minutes, or until fish flakes easily when tested with fork. Meanwhile, combine orange juice, soy sauce, vinegar and brown sugar in small saucepan; bring to boil. Remove from heat; stir in sesame oil. Arrange fish on serving platter; sprinkle green onions over fish and pour sauce over all.

SHRIMP-IN-SHELL

Makes 4 to 6 servings

1 pound medium-size raw
    shrimp, unpeeled
1/2 cup regular-strength chicken
    broth
2 tablespoons cornstarch
3 tablespoons Kikkoman Soy
    Sauce
2 teaspoons sugar
3 tablespoons vegetable oil
1 tablespoon minced fresh
    ginger root
1 large clove garlic, minced
1 red bell pepper, cut into thin
    strips
1/4 pound fresh snow peas,
    trimmed

Thoroughly rinse shrimp; devein. Let drain on several layers of paper towels. Combine chicken broth, cornstarch, soy sauce and sugar; set aside. Heat oil in hot wok or large skillet over high heat. Add ginger and garlic; stir-fry 30 seconds. Add shrimp; stir-fry 1 to 2 minutes, or until pink. Remove shrimp with slotted spoon, leaving oil in pan. Add red pepper and snow peas to same pan; stir-fry 1 minute. Stir in shrimp and soy sauce mixture. Cook and stir until mixture boils and thickens, about 1 minute.

IMPERIAL SESAME FISH

Makes 4 to 6 servings

2 teaspoons sesame seed,
    toasted
1/4 cup Kikkoman Soy Sauce
2 teaspoons distilled white
    vinegar
2 teaspoons minced fresh ginger
    root
1/2 teaspoon sugar
1/2 cup water
1 1/2 pounds fresh or thawed fish
    fillets, 1/2 to 3/4 inch thick
2 teaspoons cornstarch
1 green onion and top, chopped

Measure sesame seed into blender container; cover and process about 10 seconds, or until finely ground. Add soy sauce, vinegar, ginger and sugar; cover and process about 15 seconds, scraping down sides once. Remove 3 tablespoons sauce mixture from blender container; combine with water in small saucepan and set aside. Generously brush both sides of fish with remaining sauce. Broil about 5 minutes, or until fish flakes easily when tested with fork. Meanwhile, blend cornstarch with mixture in saucepan. Bring to boil; cook and stir until sauce thickens. Stir in green onion. Just before serving, spoon sauce over cooked fish. Serve with assorted vegetables.

Shrimp-in-Shell

SHANGHAI SWEET & SOUR FISH

Makes 4 servings

1 cup water
¼ cup brown sugar, packed
¼ cup orange juice
2½ tablespoons cornstarch
3 tablespoons Kikkoman Lite Soy Sauce
3 tablespoons vinegar
1 tablespoon tomato catsup
2 teaspoons minced fresh ginger root
1 large onion, chunked and separated
1 large green pepper, chunked
1 large carrot, sliced diagonally into very thin slices
1 pound firm fish fillets (swordfish, halibut, mahi-mahi, shark), ¾ inch thick

MICROWAVE DIRECTIONS:
Combine water, brown sugar, orange juice, cornstarch, lite soy sauce, vinegar, catsup and ginger; set aside. Combine onion, green pepper and carrot in large microwave-safe casserole. Cover and microwave on High 4 minutes. Stir in soy sauce mixture; cover and microwave on High 4 minutes. Remove from oven and let stand, covered, about 5 minutes. Meanwhile, cut fish into 1-inch pieces and place in single layer in separate small microwave-safe casserole. Cover and microwave on Medium-high (70%) 4 to 5 minutes, or until fish flakes easily when tested with fork, rotating dish once. Remove fish and add to vegetable mixture, stirring gently to combine. Serve immediately.

CHINESE TROUT

Makes 4 servings

4 medium trout (about 2 pounds), dressed
¼ cup Kikkoman Soy Sauce
2 tablespoons vegetable oil, divided
1 cup water
4 teaspoons cornstarch
1 tablespoon sugar
2 tablespoons tomato catsup
1 tablespoon Kikkoman Soy Sauce
2½ teaspoons distilled white vinegar
⅛ teaspoon crushed red pepper
½ cup sliced green onions and tops
2 teaspoons finely chopped garlic
2 teaspoons finely chopped fresh ginger root

Score both sides of trout with diagonal slashes ¼ inch deep and 1 inch apart; place in large shallow pan. Combine ¼ cup soy sauce and 1 tablespoon oil; pour over trout, turning to coat both sides well. Marinate 45 minutes, turning over once. Reserving marinade, remove trout and place on rack of broiler pan. Broil 3 inches from heat source 5 minutes on each side, or until fish flakes easily when tested with fork; brush occasionally with reserved marinade. Meanwhile, combine water, cornstarch, sugar, catsup, 1 tablespoon soy sauce, vinegar and red pepper; set aside. Heat remaining 1 tablespoon oil in saucepan over medium-high heat. Add green onions, garlic and ginger; stir-fry 2 minutes. Stir in catsup mixture. Cook and stir until sauce boils and thickens. Serve with trout.

JAPANESE RICE SALAD

Makes 6 servings

2 cups water
3 tablespoons Kikkoman Lite Soy Sauce, divided
1 cup uncooked long-grain rice, washed and
    drained
1/2 pound cooked baby shrimp
1 carrot, peeled and shredded
1/2 cup frozen green peas, thawed and drained
1/2 cup chopped green onions and tops
1 tablespoon minced fresh ginger root
1/4 cup distilled white vinegar
2 tablespoons sugar
2 teaspoons sesame seed, toasted
2 teaspoons water
    Lettuce leaves

Combine 2 cups water and 2 tablespoons lite soy
sauce in medium saucepan. Bring to boil; stir in rice.
Reduce heat and simmer, covered, 20 minutes, or
until water is absorbed. Remove from heat and cool
in pan. Rinse shrimp; drain thoroughly. Remove and
reserve 1/2 cup. Combine remaining shrimp, carrot,
peas, green onions and ginger in large bowl. Fluff
rice with fork; fold into shrimp mixture. Cover and
refrigerate until chilled. Meanwhile, measure vinegar,
sugar, remaining 1 tablespoon lite soy sauce, sesame
seed and 2 teaspoons water into jar with screw-top
lid. Cover and shake until blended and sugar
dissolves. Pour over rice mixture; toss to coat all
ingredients well. Spoon over lettuce leaves on
serving plates; sprinkle with reserved shrimp. Garnish
as desired.

副菜食譜

Sunomono Salad

SUNOMONO SALAD

Makes 4 servings

2 medium cucumbers, peeled
1 teaspoon salt
1/4 cup shredded carrot
1/4 cup distilled white vinegar
1 tablespoon sugar
2 tablespoons water
1 teaspoon sesame seed, toasted
1 1/2 teaspoons Kikkoman Soy
    Sauce
1/4 teaspoon grated fresh ginger
    root

Cut cucumbers in half lengthwise; remove seeds. Cut halves crosswise into thin slices. Place in medium bowl; sprinkle with salt and toss lightly. Let stand 45 minutes, or until no longer crisp, tossing occasionally. Drain and squeeze out excess liquid. Return cucumbers to same bowl and toss with carrot. Combine vinegar, sugar, water, sesame seed, soy sauce and ginger. Pour over cucumber mixture; toss to mix well. Cover and refrigerate until chilled. To serve, remove cucumber mixture with slotted spoon to small individual serving bowls.

STEAMED CHINESE BUNS

Makes 10 buns

1/2 pound fresh bean sprouts,
    chopped
1/4 pound medium-size raw
    shrimp, peeled, deveined
    and chopped
2 green onions and tops,
    chopped
1 clove garlic, minced
2 tablespoons cornstarch
2 tablespoons Kikkoman Soy
    Sauce
1/2 teaspoon ground ginger
1 can (7.5 oz.) refrigerated
    biscuits

MICROWAVE DIRECTIONS:
Combine bean sprouts, shrimp, green onions, garlic, cornstarch, soy sauce and ginger in 1 1/2-quart microwave-safe square dish. Microwave on High 6 minutes, until vegetables are tender-crisp, stirring once. Divide biscuit dough into 10 pieces. Flatten each piece into 3 1/2-inch round, flouring hands if dough is sticky. Place about 2 tablespoonfuls shrimp mixture in center of each round. Bring edges together to enclose filling, pinching edges to seal securely. Place half the filled buns on 6- to 7-inch microwave-safe plate. Set plate in 1 1/2-quart microwave-safe dish. Add 1/4 cup hot water to bottom of dish. Microwave on High 5 minutes, or until buns are cooked. Repeat with remaining buns. Serve hot.

CHAWAN MUSHI

Makes 4 servings

- 1/2 chicken breast, skinned and boned
- 1 tablespoon Kikkoman Soy Sauce
- 1/2 teaspoon sugar
- 3 medium-size fresh mushrooms, sliced
- 4 eggs
- 1 bottle (8 oz.) clam juice
- 1/4 cup water
- 1/2 teaspoon Kikkoman Soy Sauce
- 1/4 cup fresh or frozen green peas

Cut chicken into 1-inch square pieces. Combine 1 tablespoon soy sauce and sugar in small bowl. Stir in chicken and mushrooms, turning pieces over to coat well. Let stand 15 minutes. Beat eggs in medium bowl. Gently stir in clam juice, water and 1/2 teaspoon soy sauce. Divide chicken, mushrooms and peas equally among 4 chawan mushi cups or four 10-ounce custard cups. Pour about 1/2 cup egg mixture into each cup. Cover with chawan mushi lids or cover tops tightly with foil or plastic wrap. Carefully place filled cups on steamer rack. Pour water into large heavy pan or Dutch oven to a depth of 3/4 inch; set rack in pan. Bring water to boil; cover and steam 12 to 15 minutes, or until knife inserted into center comes out clean.

HOT ORIENTAL SALAD

Makes 6 to 8 servings

- 1 small head napa (Chinese cabbage)
- 3/4 pound fresh spinach
- 1 tablespoon vegetable oil
- 2 cloves garlic, minced
- 1/2 teaspoon ground ginger
- 2 stalks celery, cut into julienne strips
- 1/2 pound fresh mushrooms, sliced
- 2 tablespoons Kikkoman Soy Sauce

Separate and rinse napa; pat dry. Slice enough leaves crosswise into 1-inch pieces to measure 8 cups. Wash and drain spinach; tear into pieces. Heat oil in Dutch oven over medium-high heat; add garlic and ginger. Stir-fry until garlic is lightly browned. Add celery; stir-fry 2 minutes. Add cabbage and mushrooms; stir-fry 2 minutes. Add spinach; stir-fry 2 minutes longer. Stir in soy sauce and serve immediately.

Chawan Mushi

ORIENTAL TOSS

Makes 6 servings

    Boiling water
1/4 pound fresh snow peas,
    trimmed
1/4 pound fresh bean sprouts
  1 head curly leaf lettuce, washed
    and drained
1/4 pound fresh mushrooms,
    sliced
1/4 cup distilled white vinegar
  2 tablespoons sugar
  2 tablespoons Kikkoman Soy
    Sauce
  2 tablespoons water
1/2 teaspoon ground ginger

Pour enough boiling water over snow peas in small bowl to cover; let stand 10 minutes. Drain; cool under cold water and drain thoroughly. Pour boiling water over bean sprouts in colander; cool immediately under cold water and drain thoroughly. Tear lettuce into bite-size pieces; combine with snow peas, bean sprouts and mushrooms in large serving bowl. Cover and refrigerate until chilled. Meanwhile, combine vinegar, sugar, soy sauce, water and ginger until sugar dissolves. Pour desired amount of dressing over salad mixture; toss well to coat all ingredients.

HOT & SPICY GLAZED CARROTS

Makes 4 servings

2 tablespoons vegetable oil
2 dried red chili peppers
1 pound carrots, peeled and cut
  diagonally into 1/8-inch
  slices
1/4 cup Kikkoman Teriyaki Baste
  & Glaze

Heat oil in hot wok or large skillet over high heat. Add peppers and stir-fry until darkened; remove and discard. Add carrots; reduce heat to medium. Stir-fry 4 minutes, or until tender-crisp. Stir in teriyaki baste & glaze and cook until carrots are glazed. Serve immediately.

NEW YEAR FRIED RICE

Makes 6 to 8 servings

3 strips bacon, diced
3/4 cup chopped green onions and
  tops
1/3 cup diced red bell pepper
1/4 cup frozen green peas, thawed
1 egg, beaten
4 cups cold, cooked rice
2 tablespoons Kikkoman Soy
  Sauce

Cook bacon in wok or large skillet over medium heat until crisp. Add green onions, red pepper and peas; stir-fry 1 minute. Add egg and scramble. Stir in rice and cook until heated, gently separating grains. Add soy sauce; cook and stir until heated through. Serve immediately.

Top: Oriental Toss
Bottom: Hot & Spicy Glazed Carrots

Sprout-Cucumber Salad

SPROUT-CUCUMBER SALAD

Makes 8 servings

Boiling water
1 pound fresh bean sprouts
1 medium cucumber, thinly sliced
1/4 cup finely chopped green onions and tops
2 tablespoons distilled white vinegar
2 tablespoons Kikkoman Soy Sauce
2 tablespoons vegetable oil
1 1/4 teaspoons sugar
1 tablespoon sesame seed, toasted (optional)

Pour boiling water over bean sprout in colander; rinse immediately with cold water. Drain thoroughly. Arrange cucumber slices around outer edge of serving plate; set aside. Toss green onions with sprouts. Measure vinegar soy sauce, oil and sugar in jar with screw-top lid; cover and shake well Toss sprout mixture with about 2/3 of the dressing until thoroughly coated Drizzle remaining dressing over cucumbers. Spoon sprout mixture in center of serving plate; sprinkle sesame seed over all. Serve immediately

ORIENTAL TEA EGGS

Makes 8 eggs

**8 tea bags or 3 tablespoons
  loose black tea leaves**
3 cups water
1/2 cup Kikkoman Teriyaki Sauce
8 eggs, room temperature

ombine tea bags, water and teriyaki
auce in medium saucepan; add eggs.
ring to full boil over high heat. Re-
ove from heat; cover tightly and let
and 10 minutes. Remove eggs; re-
erve liquid. Place eggs under cold
nning water until cool enough to
andle. Gently tap each eggshell with
ack of metal spoon until eggs are
overed with fine cracks *(do not peel
ggs)*. Return eggs to reserved liquid.
ring to boil; reduce heat, cover and
mmer 25 minutes. Drain off liquid
nd refrigerate eggs until chilled,
bout 1 hour. Peel carefully before
erving.

CHICKEN FRIED RICE

Makes 6 to 8 servings

**1/2 pound boneless, skinless
  chicken breast**
2 tablespoons vegetable oil
**3 green onions and tops,
  chopped**
1 carrot, cut into julienne strips
1 egg, beaten
4 cups cold, cooked rice
**3 tablespoons Kikkoman Soy
  Sauce**

Cut chicken into thin strips. Heat oil in
hot wok or large skillet over high
heat. Add chicken, green onions and
carrot. Stir-fry 3 minutes, or until
chicken is browned and carrot is
tender-crisp. Add egg; cook, stirring
gently, until firm. Stir in rice and cook
until heated through, gently separating grains. Add soy sauce and stir until mixture is well blended.

Oriental Tea Eggs

SHRIMP FRIED RICE

Makes 6 servings

2 eggs
2 tablespoons water
2 tablespoons vegetable oil
3 green onions and tops,
   chopped
3 cups cold, cooked rice
1/4 pound cooked baby shrimp,
   chopped
3 tablespoons Kikkoman Soy
   Sauce

Beat eggs with water just to blend; set aside. Heat oil in hot wok or large skillet over medium heat. Add green onions; stir-fry 30 seconds. Add eggs and scramble. Stir in rice and cook until heated, gently separating grains. Add shrimp and soy sauce; cook and stir until heated through. Serve immediately.

SOY-SPINACH SALAD

Makes 4 servings

1 pound fresh spinach, washed
   and drained
4 medium-size fresh
   mushrooms, sliced
2 tablespoons vinegar
2 tablespoons water
1 tablespoon Kikkoman Soy
   Sauce
1 tablespoon vegetable oil
1 1/2 teaspoons sugar

Tear spinach into bite-size pieces place in large salad bowl and top with mushrooms. Combine vinegar, water soy sauce, oil and sugar in smal saucepan; bring to boil. Pour ho dressing over vegetables and quickly toss until spinach wilts. Serve imme diately.

Shrimp Fried Rice

BEAN SPROUT & SPINACH SALAD

Makes 4 servings

Boiling water
1 pound fresh spinach, washed
1/2 pound fresh bean sprouts
1 tablespoon sugar
4 teaspoons distilled white
    vinegar
1 tablespoon Kikkoman Soy
    Sauce
1 teaspoon sesame seed, toasted

Pour boiling water over spinach in colander; rinse immediately with cold water. Drain thoroughly and place in medium serving bowl. Repeat procedure with bean sprouts and place in same bowl. Combine sugar, vinegar, soy sauce and sesame seed; pour over vegetables and toss to combine. Cover and refrigerate at least 1 hour before serving.

PAGODA FRIED RICE

Makes 6 servings

2 strips bacon, cut crosswise
    into 1/4-inch-wide pieces
6 green onions and tops, thinly
    sliced
1 egg, beaten
4 cups cold, cooked rice
2 tablespoons Kikkoman Soy
    Sauce

Cook bacon in hot wok or large skillet over medium heat until crisp. Add green onions and stir-fry 1 minute. Add egg and scramble. Stir in rice and cook until heated through, gently separating grains. Add soy sauce and stir until mixture is well blended.

East Meets West Salad

EAST MEETS WEST SALAD

Makes 6 to 8 servings

6 cups shredded iceberg lettuce
1 large carrot, peeled and
    shredded
1 tablespoon minced fresh
    cilantro or parsley
2 tablespoons distilled white
    vinegar
4 teaspoons Kikkoman Soy
    Sauce
1 tablespoon sesame seed,
    toasted
1 tablespoon water
2 teaspoons sugar

Toss lettuce with carrot and cilantro. Measure vinegar, soy sauce, sesame seed, water and sugar into jar with screw-top lid; cover and shake well until sugar dissolves. Pour over lettuce mixture and toss lightly to combine. Serve immediately.

HUNAN-STYLE STUFFED CUCUMBERS

Makes 4 to 6 servings

- 3 cucumbers, each about 6 inches long
- 1/4 pound medium-size raw shrimp, peeled and deveined
- 3/4 pound ground pork
- 2 tablespoons Kikkoman Soy Sauce
- 2 tablespoons finely chopped green onions and tops
- 1/4 to 1/2 teaspoon crushed red pepper
- 1 clove garlic, pressed

Trim off and discard ends of cucumbers, then peel lengthwise with vegetable peeler to form stripes. Cut each cucumber crosswise into 1½-inch lengths. Scoop out and discard seeds and enough flesh, leaving about a ¼-inch shell on sides and bottoms; set aside. Mince shrimp; combine with pork, soy sauce, green onions, red pepper and garlic. Stuff cucumber shells evenly with mixture; place on steamer rack. Set rack in large pot or wok of boiling water. (Do not allow water level to reach cucumbers.) Cover and steam 12 to 15 minutes, or until pork is cooked.

Hunan-Style Stuffed Cucumber

Firecracker Salad

FIRECRACKER SALAD

Makes 6 servings

1 tablespoon sesame seed,
    toasted
2 tablespoons distilled white
    vinegar
2 teaspoons sugar
1 teaspoon minced fresh ginger
    root
4 teaspoons Kikkoman Soy
    Sauce
1 cup julienne-stripped radishes
1 cup julienne-stripped
    cucumber
4 cups finely shredded iceberg
    lettuce
1¹/₂ teaspoons minced fresh
    cilantro or parsley

Measure sesame seed, vinegar, sugar,
ginger and soy sauce into jar with
screw-top lid; cover and shake well until sugar dissolves. Combine radishes,
cucumber and 3 tablespoons dressing; cover and refrigerate 30 minutes,
stirring occasionally. Toss lettuce with
cilantro in large bowl. Pour radish
mixture and remaining dressing over
lettuce. Toss lightly to combine.

HALEAKALA RICE

Makes 6 servings

1 can (20 oz.) crushed pineapple
    in syrup
2 tablespoons butter or
    margarine
1 cup uncooked white rice
2 tablespoons chopped parsley
2 tablespoons Kikkoman Soy
    Sauce
1 teaspoon dried mint
2 tablespoons freeze-dried
    chopped chives

Drain pineapple well; reserve syrup.
Melt butter in 2-quart saucepan; stir in
rice until well coated. Add enough water to reserved pineapple syrup to
measure 2 cups; stir into rice. Add
parsley, soy sauce and mint; bring to
boil. Cover; reduce heat and simmer
35 to 40 minutes, or until liquid is absorbed. Remove from heat; stir in
pineapple and chives.

INDEX